CHENG & TSUI

"Bringing Asia to the World"™

中文聽說讀寫

INTEGRATED

Traditional Characters

CHINESE

2

Workbook

4th Edition

Yuehua Liu and Tao-chung Yao
Nyan-Ping Bi, Yaohua Shi, Liangyan Ge

Original Edition by Tao-chung Yao and Yuehua Liu
Yea-fen Chen, Liangyan Ge, Nyan-Ping Bi, Xiaojun Wang, Yaohua Shi

CHENG & TSUI

"Bringing Asia to the World"™

Copyright © 2018, 2009, 2005, 1997 by
Cheng & Tsui Company, Inc.

Fourth Edition 2018
Third Edition 2009
Second Edition 2005
First Edition 1997

21 20 19   2 3 4 5

ISBN 978-1-62291-142-4 [Fourth Edition,
Traditional Characters]

Printed in the United States of America

The *Integrated Chinese* series includes
textbooks, workbooks, character
workbooks, teacher's resources, audio,
video, and more. Visit chengtsui.co
for more information on the other
components of *Integrated Chinese*.

Publisher
JILL CHENG

Editorial Manager
BEN SHRAGGE

Editors
LEI WANG with MIKE YONG and
RANDY TELFER

Creative Director
CHRISTIAN SABOGAL

Interior Design
LIZ YATES

Illustrator
KATE PAPADAKI

Cheng & Tsui Company, Inc.
Phone (617) 988-2400 / (800) 554-1963
Fax (617) 426-3669
25 West Street
Boston, MA 02111-1213 USA
chengtsui.co

Contents

Preface

In designing the workbook exercises for Volumes 1 and 2 of *Integrated Chinese* (IC), we strove to give equal emphasis to the core language skills of listening, speaking, reading, and writing. For the new edition, we have also added *pinyin* and tone exercises for students to progressively improve their pronunciation, extra writing exercises to test their knowledge of Chinese characters, and lesson opener checklists so they can track their learning. Where appropriate, we have labeled the exercises as interpretive, interpersonal, or presentational according to the American Council on the Teaching of Foreign Languages (ACTFL) *21st Century Skills Map for World Languages*.

In addition to the print editions, the IC workbooks are also available online through the **ChengTsui Web App™** (*Essential* and *Educator Editions*). In the digital format, the exercises are presented interactively alongside the textbook content, and automatic feedback for students is provided. For more information or a free preview, visit chengtsui.co.

> ## Organizational Principles

As with the textbooks, the IC Volume 1 and 2 workbooks do not follow one pedagogical methodology, but instead blend several effective teaching approaches. When accessed through the ChengTsui Web App, the workbooks are particularly suited for differentiated instruction, blended learning, and the flipped classroom. Here are some features that distinguish the IC Volume 1 and 2 workbooks:

Form and Function
The ultimate purpose of learning any language is to be able to communicate in that language. With that goal in mind, we pay equal attention to language form and function. In addition to traditional workbook exercise types (e.g., fill-in-the-blanks, sentence completion, translation, multiple choice), we include task-based assignments that equip students to handle real-life situations using accurate and appropriate language. These exercises provide linguistic context and are written to reflect idiomatic usage.

Visual Learning
Engaging learners through rich visuals is key to our pedagogy. To build a bridge between the classroom and the target language setting, we include a range of exercises centered on authentic materials. We also include illustration-based exercises that prompt students to answer questions directly in Chinese without going through the process of translation.

Learner-Centered Tasks
We believe that workbook exercises should not only align with the textbook, but also relate to students' lives. We include exercises that simulate daily life and reference culturally relevant topics and themes, including social media and globalization. We hope such open-ended exercises will actively engage students in the subject matter, and keep them interested in the language-learning process.

Differentiated Instruction
We have designed the exercises at different difficulty levels to suit varying curricular needs. Therefore, teachers should assign the exercises at their discretion; they may use some or all of them, in any sequence. Moreover, teachers may complement the workbook exercises with their own materials, or with supplementary resources available at chengtsui.co.

Bringing It Together
Every five lessons, we provide a short cumulative review unit ("Bringing It Together") for students who wish to check their progress. These flexible units do not introduce any new learning materials, and can be included in or excluded from curricula according to individual needs.

For maximum flexibility in pacing, each lesson is divided into two parts corresponding to the lesson halves in the textbook. Teachers may spend two or three days teaching the first half and assigning students the associated exercises, then devote an equal amount of time to the second half and its exercises. Teachers may also give two separate vocabulary tests for the two readings to ease student workload.

The workbook lesson sections are as follows:

Listening Comprehension

All too often, listening comprehension is sacrificed in the formal classroom setting. Because of time constraints, students tend to focus their time and energy on mastering a few grammar points. We include a substantial number of listening comprehension exercises to remedy this imbalance. There are two categories of listening exercises; both can be done on students' own time or in the classroom. In either case, the instructor should review students' answers for accuracy.

The first group of listening exercises, which is placed at the beginning of this section, is based on the scenarios in the lesson. For the exercises to be meaningful, students should study the vocabulary list before listening to the recordings.

The second group of listening exercises is based on audio recordings of two or more short dialogues or narratives. These exercises are designed to give students extra practice on the vocabulary and grammar points introduced in the lesson. Some of the exercises, especially those that ask students to choose among several possible answers, are significantly more difficult than others. These exercises should be assigned towards the end of the lesson, after students have familiarized themselves with its content.

Audio for the workbooks (and textbooks) is accessible via the ChengTsui Web App and, for print users, at chengtsui.co/resources.

Pinyin and Tone

This new section includes exercises that ask students to identify characters with the same initials or finals and write them in *pinyin*; and to indicate the tones of characters that are pronounced similarly.

Speaking

As with Listening Comprehension, this section includes two groups of exercises. They should be assigned separately based on students' proficiency level.

To help students apply new vocabulary and grammar knowledge to meaningful communication, we first ask questions related to the dialogue or narrative, and then ask questions related to their own lives. These questions require a one- or two-sentence answer. By stringing together short questions and answers, students can construct their own short dialogues, practice in pairs, or take turns asking or answering questions.

As their confidence increases, students can progress to more difficult questions that invite them to express opinions on a number of topics. Typically, these questions are abstract, so they gradually teach students to express their opinions in longer conversations. As the school year progresses, these questions should take up more class discussion time. Because this second group of speaking exercises is quite challenging, it should be attempted only after students are well grounded in the lesson's grammar and vocabulary. Usually, this does not occur immediately after students have completed the first group of exercises.

Reading Comprehension

This section includes questions asking students to match terms, answer questions in English, or answer multiple-choice questions based on readings. There are also activities based on realia.

Writing and Grammar

Characters

These newly added exercises develop students' analytic ability by asking them to apply their knowledge of radicals and patterns. Where appropriate, space to practice writing characters is also provided.

Grammar and Usage

These drills and exercises are designed to solidify students' grasp of important grammar points. Through brief exchanges, students answer questions using specific grammatical forms, or are given sentences to complete. Because they must provide context for these exercises, students cannot treat them as simple mechanical repetition drills.

Translation

Translation has been a tool for language teaching through the ages, and positive student feedback confirms our belief in its continued importance. The exercises we have devised serve two primary functions: one, to have students apply specific grammatical structures; and two, to encourage students to build on their vocabulary. Ultimately, we believe this dual-pronged approach will enable students to realize that it takes more than just literal translation to convey an idea in a foreign language.

Writing Practice

This group of exercises is the culmination of the section, as it encourages students to express themselves through writing. Many of the topics overlap with those used in oral practice. We expect that students will find it easier to write what they have already learned to express orally.

Note: Prefaces to previous editions of IC are available at chengtsui.co.

天氣
Weather

 Check off the following items as you learn them.

Useful Expressions

[ ] Today's weather is better than yesterday's.

[ ] It's not snowing anymore.

[ ] I wonder what the weather will be like tomorrow.

[ ] I checked the weather forecast online.

Cultural Norms

[ ] Place name transliteration

[ ] Three Furnaces on the Yangtze River

[ ] Units of measurement

[ ] Twenty-four solar terms

As you progress through the lesson, note other useful expressions and cultural norms you would like to learn.

_____

_____

_____

Dialogue 1: Tomorrow's Weather Will Be Even Better!

Audio

Listening Comprehension

A Listen to the Textbook Dialogue 1 audio, then mark these statements true or false. <u>INTERPRETIVE</u>

1 _____ Yesterday's weather was very bad.

2 _____ Today's weather is better, but still a little cold.

3 _____ When Gao Xiaoyin found out that her brother had invited Bai Ying'ai to go skating with him, she didn't tell him that Bai Ying'ai had gone to New York.

4 _____ Gao Xiaoyin seems better informed than her brother about a lot of things.

5 _____ Gao Wenzhong plans to listen to music at home tomorrow.

B Listen to the Workbook Dialogue audio, then mark these statements true or false. <u>INTERPRETIVE</u>

1 _____ This conversation probably takes place at a sporting goods store.

2 _____ Bai Ying'ai and Wang Peng went skating together without inviting Li You or Gao Wenzhong.

3 _____ Among the four friends, Bai Ying'ai is the best skater.

4 _____ Gao Wenzhong plans to hire a coach for himself and Li You.

5 _____ Gao Wenzhong and Li You decide to go to the park tomorrow.

C _____ Listen to the Listening Rejoinder audio. After hearing the first speaker, select the best response from the four choices given by the second speaker. Indicate the number of your choice. <u>INTERPRETIVE</u>

Pinyin and Tone

A Identify the characters with the same finals (either *üe* or *ie*) and write them in *pinyin*.

別　約　雪　鐵　節

1 *üe:* _____

2 *ie:* _____

B Compare the tones of these characters. Indicate the tones with 1 (first tone), 2 (second tone), 3 (third tone), 4 (fourth tone), or 0 (neutral tone).

1 氣 _____ 起 _____

2 比 _____ 筆 _____

3 雪 _____ 學 _____

4 網 _____ 望 _____

Speaking

A Answer these questions in Chinese based on Textbook Dialogue 1. PRESENTATIONAL

1 How is today's weather compared with yesterday's?

2 What is Gao Wenzhong's plan for tomorrow?

3 Where did Gao Xiaoyin get the weather forecast?

4 Why does Gao Xiaoyin tell Gao Wenzhong to change his plans?

B In pairs, ask what your partner usually does when the weather is bad. INTERPERSONAL

C Check this weekend's weather forecast. Determine if the weather will be nice or not and describe what you plan to do, given the predicted conditions. PRESENTATIONAL

Reading Comprehension

A If you combine the *huá* in *huá bīng* with the *shuǐ* in *hē shuǐ*, you have *huá shuǐ*, as seen in exercise 1 below. Can you guess what the term *huá shuǐ* means? Write the characters, *pinyin*, and English equivalent of each new word formed in this way. Consult a dictionary if necessary. INTERPRETIVE

1 "滑冰"的"滑"+"喝水"的"水"

→ 滑＋水 → _____ _____ _____

2 "滑冰"的"滑"+"下雪"的"雪"

→ 滑＋雪 → _____ _____ _____

3 "學校"的"校"+"公園"的"園"

→ 校+園 → _____ _____ _____

4 "暖和"的"暖"+"天氣"的"氣"

→ 暖+氣 → _____ _____ _____

5 "約人"的"約"+"開會"的"會"

→ 約+會 → _____ _____ _____

B Read this passage, then mark the statements true or false. **INTERPRETIVE**

　　這個星期五下午，王朋約了李友星期天一起去公園滑冰。可是電視上的天氣預報說，星期天的天氣不好，會下雪。王朋就給李友打電話，告訴她星期天不去公園了。星期天上午王朋請李友來他的宿舍看電視，可是星期天的天氣很好，不但沒下雪，而且很暖和。王朋說："以後電視上說會下雪，我們就可以去公園玩兒。電視上說天氣很好，我們就只能在家看電視了。"

1 ____ The passage takes place in the summer.

2 ____ Wang Peng and Li You had to change their plans for Sunday because of the weather forecast.

3 ____ Wang Peng looked up the weather forecast online.

4 ____ The forecast predicted that it would snow.

5 ____ Wang Peng is glad that he and Li You did not go out on Sunday.

6 ____ In Wang Peng's opinion, weather forecasts are not reliable.

Read this passage, then answer the questions by circling the most appropriate choice. **INTERPRETIVE**

現在已經是一月了，可是不但不下雪，而且很暖和。大家都很高興，只有小美不太高興。她問李友："一月的天氣怎麼跟十月一樣啊？什麼時候才會冷啊？"李友不懂小美為什麼希望天氣冷，就去問白英愛，才知道小美上個星期買了一件漂亮的新大衣。

1   Which season is described in the passage?

   a   spring

   b   summer

   c   autumn

   d   winter

2   Which of the following best describes the current weather conditions?

   a   seasonably cold

   b   unseasonably warm

   c   seasonably rainy

   d   unseasonably snowy

3   Li You found Xiaomei's comments on the weather to be

   a   interesting.

   b   annoying.

   c   expected.

   d   perplexing.

4   Which of the following statements is true?

   a   Xiaomei knows both Li You and Bai Ying'ai.

   b   Xiaomei knows Li You but not Bai Ying'ai.

   c   Xiaomei knows neither Li You nor Bai Ying'ai.

   d   Xiaomei knows Bai Ying'ai but not Li You.

5   According to Bai Ying'ai, Xiaomei is quite eager to

   a   experience cold weather.

   b   experience typical October-like weather.

   c   wear her new overcoat.

   d   return her new overcoat.

Answer the following questions in English based on the weather forecast below. **INTERPRETIVE**

1　紐約這一天冷還是暖和？

_____

2　除了紐約以外，你還認識哪些城市的名字？

_____

城市	天氣	氣溫(℃)	城市	天氣	氣溫(℃)
華盛頓		34~24	新德里		35~27
紐約		32~23	德黑蘭		39~25
芝加哥		26~18	莫斯科		26~15
洛杉磯		24~17	聖彼得堡		26~15
舊金山		20~12	伊斯坦布爾		30~21
溫哥華		22~11	雅典		34~25
蒙特利爾		26~16	維也納		27~15
多倫多		28~20	日內瓦		28~12
阿卡波克		24~11	法蘭克福		25~14
巴西利亞		25~13	柏林		21~11
里約熱內盧		26~17	漢堡		20~13
布宜諾斯艾利斯		12~9	巴黎		25~15
聖地亞哥		11~6	里昂		30~18
東京		31~24	曼徹斯特		18~10
曼谷		33~25	倫敦		21~14
新加坡		29~25	斯德哥爾摩		19~12
吉隆坡		30~23	馬德里		37~17
馬尼拉		32~25	巴塞羅那		29~22
惠靈頓		13~9	米蘭		29~18
悉尼		16~8	華沙		23~12
卡拉奇		33~28	開普敦		16~6

E In addition to the weather forecast, what other useful information does this newspaper clipping feature? **INTERPRETIVE**

_____

_____

氣象小貼士

今日降旗時刻：19:45

天氣：陰有雷陣雨，偏南風2、3級，27至26°C

明日升旗時刻:4:54

天氣:多雲，偏北風1、2級，22至23°C

_____

上下班氣象

今天下班：陰有雷陣雨，偏南風2、3級，28至26°C

明天上班:多雲，偏北風1、2級，23至25°C

_____

穿衣指數

白天適宜穿薄短袖類服裝。

_____

洗車指數

未來兩天有雷陣雨，不適宜洗車。

Writing and Grammar

A Write the radical 囗 in the character 園, as in 公園. Write three more characters with the same radical, compound each of them with another character to form a disyllabic word, and then provide the meaning of each word in English (write the radical in 1).

1

3 _____

2 _____

4 _____

B Use the prompts to write some advertising copy for a promotional email, following the example.
PRESENTATIONAL

好　　便宜

我們的東西不但好，而且便宜。

1 多　　新

_____

2 好看　　好用

_____

3 男人喜歡　　女人喜歡

_____

4 大人喜歡　　小孩喜歡

_____

C Unfortunately, online reviews indicate that customers don't agree with your selling points in (B). Use the prompts to give voice to the customers' complaints. PRESENTATIONAL

好　　便宜

他們的東西不但不好，而且不便宜。

1 多　　新

_____

2 好看　　好用

_____

3 男人喜歡 ____ 女人喜歡 ____

_____

4 大人喜歡 ____ 小孩喜歡 ____

_____

D Little Wang has become environmentally conscious, and is trying to save energy any way he can. Write about what he is doing differently, following the example below. PRESENTATIONAL

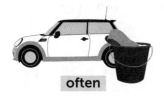 ✓ (past) ✗ (present)

often

小王以前常常洗車,現在不常洗車了。

 ✓ (past) ✗ (present)

1

_____

 ✗ (past) ✓ (present)

2

_____

 ✗ (present) ✓ (past)

3

_____

E Have any of your study habits or dietary preferences changed recently? Describe these changes by following the example. PRESENTATIONAL

我以前聽錄音，現在不聽了。

_____

_____

_____

F This is tomorrow's weather forecast for New York and Beijing. Interpret the forecast and determine, for both cities, whether it will snow and whether it will be colder or warmer than where you are. PRESENTATIONAL

1

紐約 40°F _____

2

北京 30°F _____

G Translate this sentence into Chinese. PRESENTATIONAL

The online weather forecast says that it will not only be very cold tomorrow, but it will also snow.

_____

_____

H Compare two celebrities in the same field or profession in terms of characteristics and abilities. Who is younger, taller, etc.? Who is better at singing, dancing, playing sports, etc.? PRESENTATIONAL

_____

_____

_____

_____

Dialogue 2: The Weather Here Is Awful!

Listening Comprehension

A Listen to the Textbook Dialogue 2 audio, then mark these statements true or false. **INTERPRETIVE**

1 ____ Gao Wenzhong and Bai Ying'ai are talking on the phone.

2 ____ Bai Ying'ai is looking for weather information online.

3 ____ Gao Wenzhong is moving to California for the great weather.

4 ____ Bai Ying'ai is interviewing for a job in New York because she does not like California.

5 ____ Bai Ying'ai will cut her trip short because she can't stand the local weather anymore.

B Listen to the Workbook Dialogue audio, then mark these statements true or false. **INTERPRETIVE**

1 ____ It's been raining since at least yesterday.

2 ____ The woman likes rainy weather.

3 ____ The woman is from another city.

4 ____ The man doesn't care whether the woman stays or not.

5 ____ The woman is unlikely to consider the man's suggestion.

C ____ Listen to the Listening Rejoinder audio. After hearing the first speaker, select the best response from the four choices given by the second speaker. Indicate the number of your choice. **INTERPRETIVE**

Pinyin and Tone

A Identify the characters with the same finals (either *ao* or *ou*) and write them in *pinyin*.

糟　又　糕　好　州

1 *ao:* _____

2 *ou:* _____

B Compare the tones of these characters. Indicate the tones with 1 (first tone), 2 (second tone), 3 (third tone), 4 (fourth tone), or 0 (neutral tone).

1 糟 _____   早 _____

2 夏 _____   下 _____

3 雨 _____   預 _____

4 加 _____   假 _____

Speaking

A Answer these questions in Chinese based on Textbook Dialogue 2. PRESENTATIONAL

1 How do Gao Wenzhong and Bai Ying'ai communicate with each other?

2 Why didn't Bai Ying'ai go out?

3 What is keeping Bai Ying'ai from going home?

4 Does Bai Ying'ai think that the weather in California is nice?
Does she want to go there? Why or why not?

B In pairs, ask what your partner's favorite city is and what the weather is like there in each season.
INTERPERSONAL

Reading Comprehension

A If you combine the *yǔ* in *xià yǔ* with the *yī* in *yīfu*, you have *yǔyī*, as seen in exercise 1 below. Can you guess what the word *yǔyī* means? Write the characters, *pinyin*, and English equivalent of each new word formed in this way. Consult a dictionary if necessary. INTERPRETIVE

1 "下雨"的"雨"＋"衣服"的"衣"

→ 雨＋衣 → _____ _____ _____

2 "下雨"的"雨"＋"鞋"

→ 雨＋鞋 → ＿＿＿＿＿＿ ＿＿＿＿＿＿ ＿＿＿＿＿＿

3 "一枝筆"的"筆"＋"面試"的"試"

→ 筆＋試 → ＿＿＿＿＿＿ ＿＿＿＿＿＿ ＿＿＿＿＿＿

4 "舒服"的"舒"＋"合適"的"適"

→ 舒＋適 → ＿＿＿＿＿＿ ＿＿＿＿＿＿ ＿＿＿＿＿＿

5 "寒假"的"寒"＋"冬天"的"冬"

→ 寒＋冬 → ＿＿＿＿＿＿ ＿＿＿＿＿＿ ＿＿＿＿＿＿

B Read this passage, then mark the statements true or false. **INTERPRETIVE**

　　黃先生以前在加州工作。加州冬天不冷，夏天不熱，春天和秋天更舒服。黃先生現在在紐約工作。他說紐約夏天很熱，春天和秋天也不太舒服，冬天天氣更糟糕，不但很冷，而且常常下雪。他約夏小姐這個週末去加州玩兒，夏小姐說加州天氣好是好，可是沒意思，不想去。

1 ＿＿＿ Mr. Huang used to work in California.

2 ＿＿＿ The four seasons are equally comfortable in New York.

3 ＿＿＿ In New York, winter is the worst season.

4 ＿＿＿ Mr. Huang would like to spend a weekend in California.

5 ＿＿＿ Ms. Xia declined Mr. Huang's invitation because she liked the weather in her own city better.

謝小姐是北京人，在加州工作。她的爸爸媽媽都在北京，謝小姐常常去看他們。可是她不喜歡夏天回去，因為北京的夏天很熱。謝小姐想請她爸爸媽媽夏天到加州來，可是他們說，加州好是好，但是那兒的朋友比北京少得多。他們覺得北京雖然天氣不好，可是比加州更有意思。

1 _____ 謝小姐的爸爸媽媽常常去加州。

2 _____ 謝小姐喜歡在六月或者七月回北京。

3 _____ 謝小姐的爸爸媽媽在北京有很多朋友。

4 _____ 謝小姐覺得加州夏天的天氣比北京好。

5 _____ 謝小姐的爸爸媽媽很喜歡北京。

D Read this dialogue, then mark the statements true or false. **INTERPRETIVE**

（老王和老李打電話聊天。）

老王：老李，我最近工作不忙，想去北京玩兒。

老李：現在是冬天，這兒天氣非常冷。

老王：春天呢？

老李：北京春天的天氣有的時候也很
　　　糟糕！

老王：夏天呢？

老李：夏天比春天更糟糕，不但很熱，
　　　而且常常下雨。

老王：啊，冬天不好，春天不好，夏
　　　天也不好，你不希望我去北京，
　　　對嗎？

老李：不、不，你是我最好的朋友。
　　　我希望你秋天來，因為北京秋
　　　天最舒服。

老王：那好，我秋天去。

1 ＿＿ The telephone conversation takes place in the summer.
2 ＿＿ Old Li lives in Beijing.
3 ＿＿ According to Old Li, the best season in Beijing is autumn.
4 ＿＿ It is not very cold during the winter in Beijing.
5 ＿＿ Old Li doesn't want Old Wang to come to Beijing.

E According to this sign, what takes place here?
INTERPRETIVE

_____

_____

招聘
面試處

F Answer the following questions in English based on the weather forecast. <u>INTERPRETIVE</u>

1　這是哪一個城市的天氣預報？

_____

2　哪一天最熱？

_____

3　這幾天會不會下雨？

_____

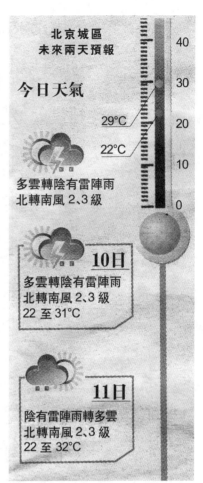

北京城區
未來兩天預報

今日天氣

29°C
22°C

40
30
20
10
0

多雲轉陰有雷陣雨
北轉南風2、3級

10日

多雲轉陰有雷陣雨
北轉南風2、3級
22 至 31°C

11日

陰有雷陣雨轉多雲
北轉南風2、3級
22 至 32°C

G Based on this lesson's Cultural Literacy section, can you find the "Three Furnaces on the Yangtze River" in the weather forecast below? What are the forecasted high temperatures in these cities? <u>INTERPRETIVE</u>

城市	天氣	最高氣溫	最低氣溫	城市	天氣	最高氣溫	最低氣溫
北京		31	22	石家莊		31	22
哈爾濱		27	18	濟南		30	22
長春		27	19	鄭州		28	20
瀋陽		28	20	合肥		29	24
天津		31	22	南京		29	24
呼和浩特		27	16	上海		35	27
烏魯木齊		37	23	武漢		30	24
西寧		24	12	長沙		33	24
銀川		29	19	南昌		30	25
蘭州		31	19	杭州		35	25
西安		35	23	福州		36	27
拉薩		20	9	南寧		33	25
成都		32	24	海口		34	26
重慶		35	25	廣州		33	26

Writing and Grammar

A Pick a character from each of the words below, compound them with another character to form a new word or phrase, then provide the meaning of each word or phrase in English. Follow the example below.

打球　　打車　　to hail a taxi

1　非常　_____　_____

2　那麼　_____　_____

3　面試　_____　_____

4　舒服　_____　_____

B Form a character by fitting the given components together as indicated, following the example below. Then provide a word or phrase in which that character appears.

日 on the left with 月 on the right: 明 as in 明天

1　力 on the left with 口 on the right: _____ as in _____

2　氵 on the left with 先 on the right: _____ as in _____

3　女 on the left with 口 on the right: _____ as in _____

4　今 on top with 心 on the bottom: _____ as in _____

5　氵 on the left with 票 on the right: _____ as in _____

C Student A is eyeing a pair of shoes she found at the mall. She loves the color, style, fit, and degree of comfort. She wants to buy them, but her friend, Student B, is only concerned about the price. Following the example below, what would you say to Student A in a diplomatic but honest way if you were Student B? PRESENTATIONAL

Student A: 這雙鞋的顏色真漂亮。

Student B: 顏色漂亮是漂亮，可是太貴了。

Lesson 11 | Weather　17

1 Student A: 這雙鞋的樣子真好看。

   Student B: 樣子 _____ ，

   _____ 。

2 Student A: 這雙鞋的大小真合適。

   Student B: 大小 _____ ，

   _____ 。

3 Student A: 這雙鞋真舒服。

   Student B: _____ ，

   _____ 。

D Little Zhang, a diehard fan of *Modern Family*, binge-watched the series over winter break. He saw some episodes on December 27 and 28, took a break to go on a trip with friends on December 29, and resumed watching the series on December 30. Continue the narrative after the given sentence, using 又 or 沒 to state whether he watched it on each of the days. **PRESENTATIONAL**

小張十二月二十七日又看了Modern Family。

十二月二十八日 _____

十二月二十九日 _____

十二月三十日 _____

E Are you a fan of *Modern Family* or any other TV show, or are you enthusiastic about a particular book series, movie, sports team, or musician? Write a description like the one above about your binge reading, watching, or listening. **PRESENTATIONAL**

_____

_____

_____

F Translate these sentences into Chinese. **PRESENTATIONAL**

1 Shoot, today is even colder than yesterday! I'd better put on my new sweater, have some hot coffee, and tell my little brother not to go outside to play.

_____

_____

2 I have three pairs of pants: one white, one black, and one brown. The white pants were $124.99 and were much more expensive than the black ones. The black ones are newer than the brown ones, but they are a little big on me. I think the brown ones fit me the best. They are not only good-looking but also inexpensive. I wore them three times last week. This week, I wore them three times again. I want to wear them three more times next week.

_____

_____

_____

_____

3 I like this school a lot. It's big and beautiful. Everyone says it's as beautiful as a park. Many students ice skate in the winter. The weather forecast said that it would be very cold and would snow next week. I hope I can go skating next weekend.

_____

_____

_____

G Narrate tomorrow's weather forecast based on the given prompts. Focus your report on possible changes in temperature and precipitation in the morning, afternoon, and late at night.
PRESENTATIONAL

_____

_____ | 10:00 am | 04:00 pm | Midnight |

_____ | 36°F | 34°F | 29°F |

_____

H Check your local weather forecast for tomorrow and report in writing whether it's predicted to rain, snow, and be warmer or colder than today. PRESENTATIONAL

_____

_____

I Choose two countries and search online to find out which country is bigger, which has a larger population (X 的人比 Y 的人多), which has a hotter summer, which has a colder winter, which has a more pleasant spring or fall, etc. Write a paragraph comparing the two countries.

PRESENTATIONAL

_____

_____

_____

_____

J Write a story in Chinese based on the four images below. Make sure your story has a beginning, middle, and end, and that the transition from one image to the next is smooth and logical.

PRESENTATIONAL

1

2

3

4

_____

_____

_____

_____

吃飯
Dining

 Check off the following items as you learn them.

Useful Expressions

[ ] Are there any tables left?

[ ] Would you like to order?

[ ] May I have _____ (a dish) please?

[ ] I'm vegetarian.

[ ] You've given me the wrong change.

Cultural Norms

[ ] Major regional cuisines

[ ] Typical staple foods

[ ] Eating utensils

[ ] Vegetarianism

As you progress through the lesson, note other useful expressions and cultural norms you would like to learn.

_____

_____

_____

Dialogue 1: Dining Out

Audio

Listening Comprehension

A   Listen to the Textbook Dialogue 1 audio, then circle the most appropriate choice. **INTERPRETIVE**

1   **When Wang Peng and Li You arrive at the restaurant,**

    a   no one greets them.

    b   there's a long wait for a table.

    c   the restaurant is not crowded at all.

    d   there is still a table available.

2   **When the waiter comes to take their order,**

    a   Wang Peng and Li You order separately.

    b   Li You asks Wang Peng to order for her.

    c   Wang Peng offers to order for Li You.

    d   Wang Peng does not want to order for Li You.

3   **Which of the following statements is true?**

    a   Wang Peng and Li You order two dishes and a soup.

    b   Wang Peng orders three dishes and a soup.

    c   Li You does not order any soup.

    d   Wang Peng orders two different soups for himself and Li You.

4   **When they order beverages,**

    a   Wang Peng asks for no ice.

    b   Wang Peng asks for extra ice.

    c   Li You asks for extra ice.

    d   Wang Peng and Li You both ask for extra ice.

5   **Which of the following statements is true?**

    a   Both Wang Peng and Li You are vegetarian.

    b   Li You is vegetarian.

    c   Wang Peng prefers vegetarian dumplings.

    d   Li You occasionally eats meat.

B   Listen to the Workbook Dialogue audio, then mark these statements true or false. **INTERPRETIVE**

1 ____   **The man and the woman are at home.**

2 ____   **The woman has completely changed her diet.**

3 ____   **The woman suggests meat dumplings because eating out as a vegetarian is too difficult.**

4 _____ The woman still doesn't eat meat at home.

5 _____ The man suggests vegetable dumplings because the woman is vegetarian.

C _____ Listen to the Listening Rejoinder audio. After hearing the first speaker, select the best response from the four choices given by the second speaker. Indicate the number of your choice. INTERPRETIVE

Pinyin and Tone

A Identify the characters with the same initials (either *j* or *x*) and write them in *pinyin*.

餃　像　些　家　精

1 *j:* _____

2 *x:* _____

B Compare the tones of these characters. Indicate the tones with 1 (first tone), 2 (second tone), 3 (third tone), 4 (fourth tone), or 0 (neutral tone).

1 都 _____ 豆 _____

2 酸 _____ 算 _____

3 碗 _____ 晚 _____

4 渴 _____ 課 _____

Speaking

A Answer these questions in Chinese based on Textbook Dialogue 1. PRESENTATIONAL

1 What is Li You's impression when she enters the restaurant?

2 Is there meat in the dumplings or the tofu dish that Li You and Wang Peng order? Why or why not?

3 What special requests does Li You make for her hot-and-sour soup?

4 Do Li You and Wang Peng order any vegetable dishes? Why or why not?

5 What drinks do Li You and Wang Peng order?

B In pairs, ask what drinks your partner usually orders at restaurants. INTERPERSONAL

C In pairs, role-play a conversation in a restaurant. The customer orders a main dish, a soup, and a drink, with special requests for the dish or drink. The waiter or waitress will recommend a dish, politely take the order, and confirm the order at the end. INTERPERSONAL

Reading Comprehension

A If you combine the *shū* in *kàn shū* with the *zhuō* in *zhuōzi*, you have *shūzhuō*, as seen in exercise 1 below. Can you guess what the word *shūzhuō* means? Write the characters, *pinyin*, and English equivalent of each new word formed in this way. Consult a dictionary if necessary. INTERPRETIVE

1 "看書"的"書"+"桌子"的"桌"

→ 書+桌 → _____ _____ _____

2 "吃飯"的"飯"+"桌子"的"桌"

→ 飯+桌 → _____ _____ _____

3 "青菜"的"菜"+"刀"

→ 菜+刀 → _____ _____ _____

4 "吃素"的"素"+"點菜"的"菜"

→ 素+菜 → _____ _____ _____

5 "喝茶"的"茶"+"飯館"的"館"

→ 茶+館 → _____ _____ _____

Read this dialogue, then answer the questions by circling the most appropriate choice.
INTERPRETIVE

李小姐：服務員，你們的家常豆腐一點兒也不好吃。酸辣湯也很糟糕。我點菜的時候告訴你我不喜歡味精，可是好像還是放了很多味精。

服務員：對不起，小姐，可是菜你都吃完了……大家都說我們飯館兒的菜很不錯，有的菜六點就賣完了。

李小姐：你自己覺得這兒的菜怎麼樣？

服務員：我不知道。

李小姐：你怎麼不知道？你在這兒工作，不在這兒吃飯嗎？

服務員：我真的不知道，因為我和別的服務員都去別的飯館兒吃飯。

1 **Why didn't Miss Li like the soup?**

   a   It was too hot.

   b   It was too sour.

   c   It was not cooked in the way she wanted.

2 **In commenting on the food, what does the waiter suggest?**

   a   Since Miss Li finished the food, it must have been okay.

   b   Since Miss Li didn't finish the food, it must not have been good.

   c   Some dishes had sold out, because they were cheap.

3 **The waiter tries to defend his restaurant by saying that**

   a   its dishes have sold out very quickly.

   b   customers have to come early to get a table.

   c   some dishes aren't fresh because they have to be prepared early.

4 Miss Li had assumed that

 a the waiter does not have meals at the restaurant, even though he works there.

 b the waiter eats at the restaurant every day, since he works there.

 c the waiter eats lunch at the restaurant on his days off.

5 How does the waiter like the food at the restaurant where he works?

 a He doesn't like it, even though he eats it every day.

 b He likes it, even though he isn't usually allowed to eat there.

 c He doesn't have an opinion because he's never eaten at the restaurant.

C Read this passage, then mark the sentences true or false. INTERPRETIVE

王朋和李友昨天晚上六點到一家飯館兒吃
飯。他們要了兩杯可樂。王朋點了一盤肉和一
盤餃子。李友一點兒肉也不吃，所以只要了一
盤豆腐。兩杯可樂很快就來了，可是到了七點
半一盤菜都沒上。王朋問服務員：「我們的菜
做好了嗎？」服務員說：「你們現在餓了嗎？」王
朋和李友都說：「我們都餓了。」服務員告訴他
們：「我們飯館兒跟別的飯館兒不一樣。要是你
不太餓，你會覺得我們的菜一點兒也不好吃。
要是你餓了，才會覺得我們的菜特別好吃。所
以我得等你們很餓了才上菜。」

1 ____ Li You ordered a cola and a vegetarian dish.

2 ____ Wang Peng and Li You waited for their drinks for a long time.

3 ____ At 7:30, not even a single dish had arrived.

4 ____ We can assume that Wang Peng and Li You will visit this restaurant again soon.

D Based on the passage in (C), circle the most appropriate choice. INTERPRETIVE

1 According to the waiter, this restaurant is unique in that

 a its delicious food makes customers feel even hungrier.

 b its customers can never have enough of its delicious food.

 c its food is delicious only to customers who are hungry.

2 According to the waiter, he had to

    a   wait for Wang Peng and Li You to become really hungry.

    b   wait on other hungry customers first.

    c   eat first because he was hungry.

E Look at this menu and answer the questions. **INTERPRETIVE**

   1 What can you order from this menu if you are vegetarian?

   2 How much does the hot-and-sour soup cost?

No 0032733 **价目表**

品　　　名	單價	數　　　量	金額
招牌鍋貼	4		
韭菜鍋貼	4		
辣味鍋貼	5		
招牌水餃	5		
韭菜水餃	5		
辣味水餃	5		
素水餃	5		
鮮蝦水餃	7		
湯類			
酸辣湯	25		
玉米濃湯	25		
旗魚丸湯	25		
原汁豆漿	15		
純黑豆漿	15		
米漿	15		

合計 : _____

Writing and Grammar

A 孩子 and 褲子 contain the character 子. Provide three more disyllabic words from this lesson that contain 子, along with their *pinyin* and English meanings.

1 _____ _____ _____

2 _____ _____ _____

3 _____ _____ _____

B Describe the images by writing the appropriate numbers, measure words, and nouns, following the example below. Use each measure word only once. PRESENTATIONAL

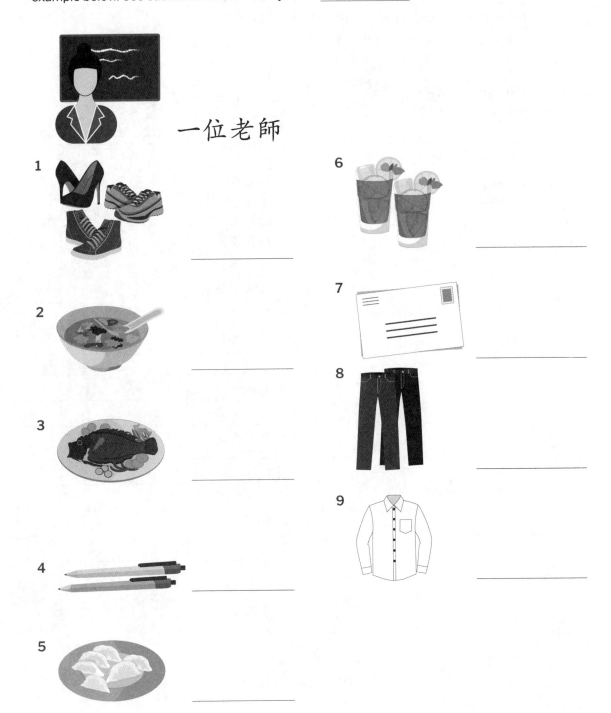

一位老師

1 _____

2 _____

3 _____

4 _____

5 _____

6 _____

7 _____

8 _____

9 _____

C This past winter break, Little Gao was too busy to do anything and too broke to buy anything. Based on the images, use 一⋯⋯也／都⋯⋯不／沒⋯⋯ to describe what he was not able to do over break. Follow the example below. PRESENTATIONAL

寒假小高一個電影也／都沒看。

1

_____

2

_____

3

_____

D Mr. Li is not feeling well and has no appetite. Based on the images, use 一…也/都… 不/沒… to describe what he doesn't want to eat or drink. **PRESENTATIONAL**

李先生不舒服，一點兒茶都不想喝。

1

_____

2

_____

3

_____

4

_____

E You just received your latest test scores and are trying to motivate yourself to improve your grades. List below in Chinese what you need to do more and less of in order to reach your goal. **PRESENTATIONAL**

多…   少…

_____   _____

_____   _____

_____   _____

F When Little Wang's mother says 要是功課沒做好，就不能玩兒 she really means 功課做好了，才能玩兒。 Based on this example, rephrase the following sentences so that Little Wang can better understand them. **PRESENTATIONAL**

1 要是飯沒吃完，就不能玩兒。

_____

2 要是漢字沒寫對，就不能玩兒。

_____

3 要是錄音沒聽懂，就不能玩兒。

_____

4 要是考試沒準備好，就不能玩兒。

_____

G Translate these sentences into Chinese. **PRESENTATIONAL**

1 **Student A:** Do you use MSG when you cook?

_____

Student B: No, I don't. Not even a little.

_____

2 **Student A:** Eat some more. Aren't you hungry?

_____

Student B: I'm hungry, but I'm vegetarian.

_____

Student A: Really? I'll make some vegetable dumplings. They'll be ready in no time.

_____

Student B: Great, thanks!

_____

Dialogue 2: At the Dining Hall

Listening Comprehension

A Listen to the Textbook Dialogue 2 audio, then mark these statements true or false. INTERPRETIVE

1 ____ There isn't anything good to eat at the dining hall.

2 ____ The sweet-and-sour fish is very tasty.

3 ____ Wang Peng doesn't like the chef's recommendation.

4 ____ Wang Peng doesn't have any cash on him.

5 ____ The chef shortchanges Wang Peng.

B Listen to the Workbook Dialogue audio, then circle the most appropriate choice. INTERPRETIVE

1 Who's cooking tonight?

   a The woman will do all the cooking tonight.

   b The woman will do most of the cooking tonight.

   c The man will do all the cooking tonight.

   d The man will do most of the cooking tonight.

2 Who wants soup?

   a the man

   b the woman

   c both the man and the woman

   d neither the man nor the woman

3 Which of the following statements is true?

   a The man will make the soup.

   b The woman will make the soup.

   c The man and the woman will make the soup together.

   d The man and the woman will each make their own soup.

4 Why does the woman offer to make the soup?

   a The man doesn't know how to make it.

   b She doesn't like how the man makes it.

   c She wants to help.

   d The man doesn't feel like making soup.

C ____ Listen to the Listening Rejoinder audio. After hearing the first speaker, select the best response from the four choices given by the second speaker. Indicate the number of your choice. INTERPRETIVE

Pinyin and Tone

A Identify the characters with the same finals (either *uan* or *an*) and write them in *pinyin*.

暖 飯 酸 拌 盤

1 *uan:* _____

2 *an:* _____

B Compare the tones of these characters. Indicate the tones with 1 (first tone), 2 (second tone), 3 (third tone), 4 (fourth tone), or 0 (neutral tone).

1 湯 _____ 糖 _____

2 甜 _____ 天 _____

3 燒 _____ 少 _____

4 拌 _____ 辦 _____

Speaking

A Answer these questions in Chinese based on Textbook Dialogue 2. **PRESENTATIONAL**

1 How does the chef describe the sweet-and-sour fish?

2 Does Wang Peng order the beef braised in soy sauce?

3 What does Wang Peng finally order?

4 How much in change does the chef give Wang Peng? Why?

B In pairs, ask how much your partner usually spends on lunch. **INTERPERSONAL**

C In pairs, role-play a conversation. Ask your partner (a waiter in a restaurant) what the total cost of your order is. He/she tells you the price; you pay with a large bill and ask for change. He/she gives you the wrong change, either too much or too little. Politely explain why the change he/she gave you is incorrect. **INTERPERSONAL**

Reading Comprehension

A If you combine the *mǐ* in *mǐfàn* with the *cù* in *tángcùyú*, you have *mǐcù*, as seen in exercise 1 below. Can you guess what the word *mǐcù* means? Write the characters, *pinyin*, and English equivalent of each new word formed in this way. Consult a dictionary if necessary. INTERPRETIVE

1 "米飯"的"米"＋"糖醋魚"的"醋"

→ 米＋醋 → ＿＿＿＿＿ ＿＿＿＿＿ ＿＿＿＿＿

2 "酸辣湯"的"酸"＋"下雨"的"雨"

→ 酸＋雨 → ＿＿＿＿＿ ＿＿＿＿＿ ＿＿＿＿＿

3 "金"＋"糖醋魚"的"魚"

→ 金＋魚 → ＿＿＿＿＿ ＿＿＿＿＿ ＿＿＿＿＿

4 "涼拌"的"涼"＋"鞋"

→ 涼＋鞋 → ＿＿＿＿＿ ＿＿＿＿＿ ＿＿＿＿＿

5 "喝水"的"水"＋"牛肉"的"牛"

→ 水＋牛 → ＿＿＿＿＿ ＿＿＿＿＿ ＿＿＿＿＿

B Read this dialogue, then mark the statements true or false. INTERPRETIVE

李先生：請問，你們的紅燒牛肉怎麼樣？

服務員：好吃極了。

李先生：你們的家常豆腐好吃不好吃？

服務員：家常豆腐比紅燒牛肉更好吃。

李先生：那你們的糖醋魚呢？

服務員：糖醋魚比家常豆腐更好吃。

李先生：你們的菜都好吃，那我點什麼呢？還是給我一盤紅燒牛肉吧。

服務員：好，紅燒牛肉比糖醋魚更好吃。

李先生：你剛才說家常豆腐比紅燒牛肉更好吃。算了吧，我不點菜了。我去別的飯館吧。

服務員：先生，為什麼？

李先生：因為你不知道哪個菜好吃。

1 ___ Mr. Li is very familiar with the menu.

2 ___ The waiter believes that beef braised in soy sauce is the most delicious dish on the menu.

3 ___ Mr. Li is vegetarian.

4 ___ In the end, Mr. Li decides not to eat at the restaurant.

C Based on the dialogue in (B), circle the most appropriate choice. **INTERPRETIVE**

1 Which of the following statements is true?

 a The waiter's enthusiasm for the food at his restaurant is genuine.

 b The waiter thinks that the sweet-and-sour fish tastes best.

 c The waiter tries to rush Mr. Li into making a quick order.

2 Mr. Li decides to eat elsewhere because

 a he loses confidence in the waiter's recommendations.

 b he loses count of the number of dishes he orders.

 c he thinks that the service is far too slow.

Read this passage, then complete the task. INTERPRETIVE

　　小謝和小張剛打完球，現在又餓又渴。
他們走進一家餐廳，想點些吃的和喝的東西。
可是他們兩個人一共只有三十二塊五毛錢。
他們最少得點一個素菜、一個葷菜 (hūncài)（有
肉的菜）、一碗湯、兩碗飯，兩個人還得喝點
東西。不過小謝不吃辣的菜，小張不能喝茶或
者咖啡。要是你是小謝或者小張，你怎麼辦？
下邊是餐廳的菜單，請你看一下，然後幫小謝
和小張點些吃的和喝的。

菜單

素餃子	9.50	（一盤）
牛肉餃子	12.50	（一盤）
紅燒牛肉	15.50	
糖醋牛肉	15.50	
紅燒魚	12.50	
糖醋魚	12.50	
*家常豆腐	9.50	
紅燒豆腐	9.50	
*涼拌黃瓜	6.50	
白菜豆腐湯	3.00	（兩人份）
白飯	1.00	
可樂	1.50	
綠茶	1.50	
紅茶	1.50	
咖啡	2.50	

*=辣的菜

看了菜單以後，現在請你幫小謝和小張點菜。

點菜單

第一道菜：＿＿＿＿＿＿＿＿＿　$＿＿＿＿＿＿＿＿＿

第二道菜：＿＿＿＿＿＿＿＿＿　$＿＿＿＿＿＿＿＿＿

第三道菜：＿＿＿＿＿＿＿＿＿　$＿＿＿＿＿＿＿＿＿

湯：＿＿＿＿＿＿＿＿＿＿＿＿　$＿＿＿＿＿＿＿＿＿

喝的東西：＿＿＿＿＿＿＿＿　$＿＿＿＿＿＿＿＿＿

飯：＿＿＿＿＿＿＿＿＿＿＿＿　$＿＿＿＿＿＿＿＿＿

$＿＿＿＿＿＿＿＿＿

E Read this passage, then answer the first two questions in English and the third question in Chinese.
INTERPRETIVE

　　小夏渴極了，也餓極了。他走進飯館，想點一杯涼涼的、甜甜的可樂。可是，上個星期醫生告訴他得少喝甜的東西。他又想點茶或者咖啡，也不行，因為喝了會讓他緊張。那來碗酸辣湯吧！可是醫生說他一點兒辣的都不能吃。算了，算了，多喝水吧！小夏想點牛肉，不過，最近牛肉好像有問題。那還是吃魚吧！可是服務員告訴他魚賣完了。糟糕！那吃什麼呢？ 最後，小夏點了一盤素餃子、一盤豆腐、一盤涼拌黃瓜。吃完以後，小夏覺得不夠，還覺得餓。要是你是小夏，這個時候你怎麼辦？

1 List on the left all the drinks and dishes that Little Xia wished to order but didn't, and explain on the right why he didn't.

＿＿＿＿＿＿＿＿＿＿＿　＿＿＿＿＿＿＿＿＿＿＿＿＿＿＿＿

＿＿＿＿＿＿＿＿＿＿＿　＿＿＿＿＿＿＿＿＿＿＿＿＿＿＿＿

_____ _____

_____ _____

_____ _____

2 What did Little Xia end up having at the restaurant? Do you like his choices? Why or why not?

_____

3 Answer the question raised at the end of the passage.

_____

F Look at today's menu, then write down the price of the cucumber salad. INTERPRETIVE

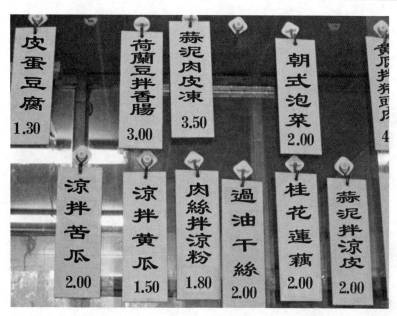

G Can students use meal cards at this particular cafeteria? INTERPRETIVE

_____

_____

A Write the common component and the characters, and provide their *pinyin*. Then write one more character that has the same component in it, and provide its *pinyin* and the meaning in English (write the common component in 1).

精　清

1 _____

2 _____

3 _____

4 _____

B Form a character by fitting the given components together as indicated, following the example below. Then provide a word, a phrase, or a short sentence in which that character appears.

口 on the left with 加 on the right: 咖 as in 咖啡.

1　口 on top with 貝 on the bottom: _____ as in _____

2　米 on the left with 青 on the right: _____ as in _____

3　食 on the left with 我 on the right: _____ as in _____

4　氵 on the left with 青 on the right: _____ as in _____

5　氵 on the left with 每 on the right: _____ as in _____

C Everyone's tastes and dietary restrictions are different. What requests do you personally make when placing an order at a restaurant? Form several requests using 多放 or 少放 in your answers. PRESENTATIONAL

多放 少放

_____   _____

_____   _____

_____   _____

D Place orders based on the images, following the example below. **PRESENTATIONAL**

 服務員，來兩碗米飯。

1

_____

2

_____

3

_____

4

_____

E When 酸辣湯 comes to mind, many people who like it will immediately think of the expression 酸酸的、辣辣的，很好喝. What do the following bring to mind? PRESENTATIONAL

1 糖醋魚：_____

2 涼拌豆腐：_____

3 冰咖啡：_____

F Answer these questions according to your own circumstances. INTERPERSONAL

1 Q: 你覺得中國菜好吃還是美國菜好吃？

A: _____

2 Q: 你喜歡吃青菜還是吃肉？

A: _____

3 Q: 天氣熱的時候，你喜歡喝什麼？

A: _____

4 Q: 你平常先喝湯再吃飯，還是先吃飯再喝湯？

A: _____

5 Q: 你能吃辣的嗎？

A: _____

6 Q: 要是你不能吃味精，你跟服務員說什麼？

A: _____

Translate these sentences into Chinese. **PRESENTATIONAL**

1 **Student A:** We just finished our exam. I asked Little Li to have dinner with us tomorrow.

_____

Student B: Great! What should we make, then?

_____

Student A: He likes to eat meat. We'll make beef braised in soy sauce and sweet-and-sour fish. How about it?

_____

Student B: You're vegetarian. I'll make some vegetarian dumplings and a cucumber salad.

_____

Student A: Good. Little Li likes vegetarian dumplings and cucumber salad, too.

_____

2 Yesterday was Little Wang's birthday. I treated him to dinner. We went to a Chinese restaurant. When we arrived, there wasn't even a single customer. The waiter asked us what we wanted to eat. I ordered a plate of dumplings. Little Wang said he was hungry and thirsty. He ordered a cola, a tofu dish, and sweet-and-sour fish. The waiter wanted us to order one more dish. We said we'd already ordered enough food. But the dumplings were sold out and the fish was too sour. The waiter not only served the food slowly but also gave the wrong change. The service there was really terrible. We'd better not go there again in the future.

_____

_____

_____

_____

_____

_____

H Suppose that you're a restaurant manager. Make a flyer to promote your specials of the day. The flyer must include one spicy dish, one meat dish, one vegetable dish, and one soup. Make sure that the flyer appropriately promotes your dishes, and don't forget to mention that you don't put any MSG in your dishes. **PRESENTATIONAL**

I   Write a story based on the four images below. Make sure that your story has a beginning, middle, and end, and that the transition from one picture to the next is smooth and logical. PRESENTATIONAL

1

中國餐廳

2

3

?!

4

_____

_____

_____

_____

_____

問路
Asking Directions

 Check off the following items as you learn them.

Useful Expressions

[ ] Where are you off to?

[ ] Where is _____ (a place)?

[ ] I don't know how to get there.

[ ] I have no sense of direction.

[ ] Turn left/right.

Cultural Norms

[ ] Feng shui

[ ] Four Symbols

[ ] Chinatown

[ ] Casual greetings

[ ] Urban planning

As you progress through the lesson, note other useful expressions and cultural norms you would like to learn.

_____

_____

_____

Dialogue 1: Where Are You Off To?

Audio

Listening Comprehension

A Listen to the Textbook Dialogue 1 audio, then circle the most appropriate choice. **INTERPRETIVE**

1 **Teacher Chang asks Bai Ying'ai where she is going because**

   a   Teacher Chang is nosy.

   b   this is a common way to greet someone.

   c   Teacher Chang needs to know where Bai Ying'ai is going.

   d   Bai Ying'ai looks lost.

2 **Does Bai Ying'ai know how to get to the computer center?**

   a   No, Bai Ying'ai doesn't know how to get to the computer center.

   b   No, Bai Ying'ai has forgotten how to get to the computer center.

   c   No, Bai Ying'ai has no idea where the computer center is.

   d   No, and Teacher Chang doesn't know how to get to the computer center either.

3 **Which description of the campus is correct?**

   a   The library is between the computer center and the student activity center.

   b   The student activity center is between the library and the computer center.

   c   The computer center is between the library and the student activity center.

   d   The computer center is between Wang Peng's dorm and the library.

4 **Teacher Chang and Bai Ying'ai will walk together because**

   a   Teacher Chang enjoys Bai Ying'ai's company.

   b   Teacher Chang's destination is not far away from Bai Ying'ai's.

   c   Bai Ying'ai asks Teacher Chang to walk with her.

   d   they haven't seen each other for a long time.

B Listen to the Workbook Dialogue audio, then mark these statements true or false. **INTERPRETIVE**

1 ____ **The woman doesn't know where the athletic field is.**

2 ____ **The man doesn't know where the computer center is.**

3 ____ **The woman is on her way to the computer center.**

4 ____ **The athletic field is between the library and the computer center.**

C ____ Listen to the Listening Rejoinder audio. After hearing the first speaker, select the best response from the four choices given by the second speaker. Indicate the number of your choice. **INTERPRETIVE**

Pinyin and Tone

A Identify the characters with the same finals (either *eng* or *ong*) and write them in *pinyin*.

動　冷　空　冬　更

1 *eng:* _____

2 *ong:* _____

B Compare the tones of these characters. Indicate the tones with 1 (first tone), 2 (second tone), 3 (third tone), 4 (fourth tone), or 0 (neutral tone).

1 場 _____ 常 _____

2 遠 _____ 園 _____

3 離 _____ 裡 _____

4 方 _____ 放 _____

Speaking

A Answer these questions in Chinese based on Textbook Dialogue 1. PRESENTATIONAL

1 Where does Bai Ying'ai want to go?

2 Which is farther from the classroom, the computer center or the athletic field?

3 Where is the computer center?

4 Why does Teacher Chang offer to go together with Bai Ying'ai?

B Draw a simple map of your school's campus and indicate where the library, student activity center, computer lab, athletic field, and your Chinese classroom are in relation to each other. In pairs, pretend you are a new student and ask your partner for directions to the school library and the student activity center. INTERPERSONAL

Reading Comprehension

A If you combine the *jìn* in *yuǎnjìn* with the *lù* in *gāosù gōnglù*, you have *jìnlù*, as seen in exercise 1 below. Can you guess what the word *jìnlù* means? Write the characters, *pinyin*, and English equivalent of each new word formed in this way. Consult a dictionary if necessary. **INTERPRETIVE**

1 "遠近"的"近"+"高速公路"的"路"

→ 近+路 → ＿＿＿＿＿＿ ＿＿＿＿＿＿ ＿＿＿＿＿＿

2 "運動"的"動"+"生詞"的"詞"

→ 動+詞 → ＿＿＿＿＿＿ ＿＿＿＿＿＿ ＿＿＿＿＿＿

3 "遠近"的"遠"+"電視"的"視"

→ 遠+視 → ＿＿＿＿＿＿ ＿＿＿＿＿＿ ＿＿＿＿＿＿

4 "遠近"的"近"+"電視"的"視"

→ 近+視 → ＿＿＿＿＿＿ ＿＿＿＿＿＿ ＿＿＿＿＿＿

5 "書店"的"店"+"服務員"的"員"

→ 店+員 → ＿＿＿＿＿＿ ＿＿＿＿＿＿ ＿＿＿＿＿＿

B Read this passage, then mark the statements true or false. **INTERPRETIVE**

　　小錢的家離學校很遠。每天早上，他都得先坐公共汽車，然後換地鐵，才能到學校。因為每天去學校上課都得花很多時間，所以他覺得很累，希望能換一個學校。他希望新學校離家近一點兒。

1 ___ Little Qian lives in a dorm.

2 ___ Little Qian's home is near a subway line.

3 ___ Little Qian takes the bus to the subway.

4 ___ Little Qian doesn't mind the commute.

5 ___ Little Qian would like to go to a different school if possible.

C Read this passage, then mark the statements true or false. **INTERPRETIVE**

藍先生早上想到學校運動場去運動，可是他不知道運動場在哪兒。八點，他在圖書館前邊看到李友，問李友運動場在哪兒，比書店近還是比書店遠。李友告訴他運動場沒有書店那麼遠。藍先生走到了書店，可是沒有看到運動場。書店的售貨員告訴他，運動場就在電腦中心的旁邊。藍先生到了電腦中心，也沒找到運動場，因為他不知道學校有兩個書店和兩個電腦中心。九點藍先生又回到了圖書館。李友問：「您去運動場運動了嗎？」藍先生說：「不運動了，我今天已經走夠了。」

1 ___ Mr. Lan doesn't know the campus well.

2 ___ Mr. Lan and Li You go to the library together.

3 ___ Li You tells Mr. Lan that he should see the athletic field before the bookstore.

4 ___ It is likely that Li You was at the library for at least an hour.

5 ___ In the end, Mr. Lan opts not to go to the athletic field because he has had enough exercise already trying to find it.

6 ___ Mr. Lan doesn't find the athletic field because of a miscommunication.

D Look at this map, then answer the question in Chinese. **INTERPERSONAL**

第一教學樓離圖書館近還是第二教學樓離圖書館近？

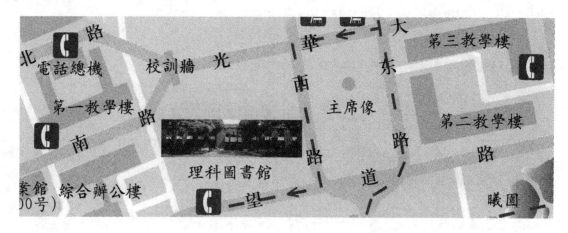

_____

_____

Writing and Grammar

A Use the second character in each word to form a different word, then provide the meaning of the new word in English.

1 聽說 _____ _____

2 旁邊 _____ _____

3 中間 _____ _____

4 書店 _____ _____

B Based on each pair of images, write two sentences to describe what Little Gao thinks. Follow the example below. **PRESENTATIONAL**

 delicious

小高覺得餃子比米飯好吃。
小高覺得米飯沒有餃子好吃。

1 ✅  中文 ❌ English difficult

_____

_____

2 ✅ 🩰 ❌ ⚫ fun/interesting

_____

_____

3 ✅ ☕ ❌ Cola expensive

_____

_____

C List the activities that students can do at the student center at your school, following the example below. **PRESENTATIONAL**

學生可以到學生活動中心去運動。

1 _____

2 _____

3 _____

4 _____

5 _____

D Imagine that you are a campus planner. Make a plan for an ideal school. Where would you situate the library, classrooms, dorms, teachers' offices, computer lab, and athletic facilities in relation to one another? Explain why in Chinese. PRESENTATIONAL

_____

_____

_____

_____

_____

_____

E Translate these sentences into Chinese. PRESENTATIONAL

1 **Student A:** Is the bookstore between the student center and the athletic field?

_____

  Student B: No, it's inside that dorm.

_____

2 **Student A:** I heard the park isn't far away from here. Do you know how to get there?

_____

  Student B: Yes, I do. I'm heading there, too. Let's go together.

_____

  Student A: Great!

_____

Dialogue 2: Going to Chinatown

Listening Comprehension

A Listen to the Textbook Dialogue 2 audio, then circle the most appropriate choice. INTERPRETIVE

1 **Who has been to Chinatown before?**

a Both Wang Peng and Gao Wenzhong have been to Chinatown many times.

b Wang Peng has been to Chinatown before.

c Neither Gao Wenzhong nor Wang Peng has been to Chinatown before.

d Gao Wenzhong has been to Chinatown before.

2 **Do they have a map?**

a Yes, Wang Peng has a map in his car.

b Yes, Gao Wenzhong brings a map.

c No, Gao Wenzhong forgets to bring the map.

d No, Wang Peng doesn't need a map.

3 **Where do they end up?**

a in Chinatown

b back at Wang Peng's place

c at a traffic light

d in Little Tokyo

B Listen to the Workbook Dialogue audio, then circle the most appropriate choice. INTERPRETIVE

1 **Where did the speakers think they were heading to?**

a a restaurant in Beijing

b a restaurant in Tokyo

c a restaurant called Beijing

d a restaurant called Tokyo

2 **The woman becomes worried they won't be able to get a seat at the restaurant because**

a the restaurant is still another six blocks away.

b it is Friday and a lot of people are dining out.

c the restaurant doesn't take reservations.

d no one answers the phone at the restaurant.

3 **They end up having Japanese food because**

a they had Chinese food last weekend.

b they are going to Tokyo soon.

c the man called the wrong restaurant.

d the Japanese restaurant is closer.

C _____ Listen to the Listening Rejoinder audio. After hearing the first speaker, select the best response from the four choices given by the second speaker. Indicate the number of your choice. INTERPRETIVE

Pinyin and Tone

A Identify the characters with the same finals (either *uo* or *ou*) and write them in *pinyin*.

過　夠　國　肉　左　豆

1 *uo:* _____

2 *ou:* _____

B Compare the tones of these characters. Indicate the tones with 1 (first tone), 2 (second tone), 3 (third tone), 4 (fourth tone), or 0 (neutral tone).

1 拿 _____ 那 _____　　3 燈 _____ 等 _____

2 男 _____ 南 _____　　4 左 _____ 做 _____

Speaking

A Answer these questions in Chinese based on Textbook Dialogue 2. PRESENTATIONAL

1 Why didn't Wang Peng know where Chinatown was?

2 Did Wang Peng and Gao Wenzhong have a map with them? Why or why not?

3 What directions did Gao Wenzhong give Wang Peng to get to Chinatown?

4 Why didn't they make a turn at the fourth intersection?

5 Did Wang Peng and Gao Wenzhong arrive in Chinatown? Why or why not?

B In pairs, ask your partner if he/she has ever been to a Chinatown. If so, ask what he/she did there. If not, ask how he/she would like to spend a day in Chinatown. INTERPERSONAL

C Tell your classmates how to get to your place from school. Draw a map to illustrate the route. PRESENTATIONAL

A If you combine the *zuǒ* in *zuǒbian* with *shǒu*, you have *zuǒshǒu*, as seen in exercise 1 below. Can you guess what the word *zuǒshǒu* means? Write the characters, *pinyin*, and English equivalent of each new word formed in this way. Consult a dictionary if necessary. <u>INTERPRETIVE</u>

1 "左邊"的"左"＋"手"

→ 左＋手 → _____ _____ _____

2 "右邊"的"右"＋"手"

→ 右＋手 → _____ _____ _____

3 "前面"的"前"＋"門"

→ 前＋門 → _____ _____ _____

4 "紅綠燈"的"紅"＋"冰茶"的"茶"

→ 紅＋茶 → _____ _____ _____

5 "紅綠燈"的"綠"＋"冰茶"的"茶"

→ 綠＋茶 → _____ _____ _____

B Mark the statements true or false according to the campus map. <u>INTERPRETIVE</u>

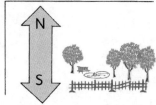

宿舍

圖書館

1 _____ 學生宿舍的東邊有一個公園。

2 _____ 圖書館在學生宿舍的南邊。

3 _____ 學生宿舍在運動場的西邊。

4 _____ 公園的北邊有公共汽車站。

C Read this passage and answer the questions. **INTERPRETIVE**

老李去過中國城買東西、吃中國飯，但是每次都是坐朋友的車去。上個週末老李自己開車到中國城去，但是忘了帶手機，看不了地圖，所以走錯了。他想回家去拿手機，可是找不到回家的路。他想問朋友，可是沒有手機，也不能問。老李很緊張，就到旁邊的飯館兒問。飯館兒的師傅告訴他一直往東開，到第三個紅綠燈就能看到中國城了。

1 What has Old Li done in Chinatown in the past?

_____

2 How did he get to Chinatown in the past?

_____

3 Why couldn't he locate Chinatown last weekend?

_____

4 Why didn't he go home to get his cell phone?

_____

5 Why didn't he call someone for help?

_____

6 How did he finally find Chinatown?

_____

D Read this passage and answer the questions. **INTERPRETIVE**

快考試了，我得去書店買書復習復習，但我沒去過書店。小白說走到那裡太慢，開車很快就能到。她說從學校出去，先上大學路，一直往南開，到第一個紅綠燈往東開。然後到了第一個路口往左一拐就會看到路的右邊有一家活動中心。再往前走，就會看到路的左邊有一家鞋店，書店就在鞋店的北邊。

1 What does the narrator want to buy? Why?

_____

2 According to Little Bai, is it more convenient to drive or walk to the narrator's destination?

_____

3 Based on Little Bai's directions, draw a map of the route to the narrator's destination and indicate all the landmarks.

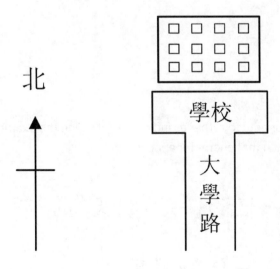

E Look at this map and answer the question in Chinese. **INTERPRETIVE**

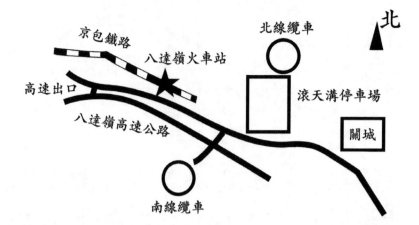

Is the train station to the north, east, south, or west of the highway?

_____

Writing and Grammar

A Write the common radical and its meaning in English, then write the two characters and their meanings in English. Provide another character with the same radical, a two-syllable word in which the character is used, and the meaning of the word in English (write the common radical in 1).

城　地

1 _____

3 _____

2 _____

4 _____ _____

B Form a character by fitting the given components together as indicated, following the example below. Then provide a word or phrase in which that character appears.

左邊一個"日"，右邊一個"月"是"明天"的"明"。

1 左邊一個"土"，右邊一個"也"是 _____
的 _____ 。

2 外邊一個"門"，裡邊一個"日"是 ＿＿＿＿＿＿＿ 的 ＿＿＿＿＿。

3 上邊一個"合"，下邊一個"手"是 ＿＿＿＿＿＿＿ 的 ＿＿＿＿＿。

4 上邊一個"山"，下邊一個"山"是 ＿＿＿＿＿＿＿ 的 ＿＿＿＿＿。

5 上邊一個"口"，下邊一個"八"是 ＿＿＿＿＿＿＿ 的 ＿＿＿＿＿。

C Form questions-and-answers based on your own experience, following the prompts and the example below. **PRESENTATIONAL**

Q: 你吃過涼拌黃瓜嗎？

A: 我吃過。

Q: 你覺得涼拌黃瓜好吃嗎？

A: 我覺得涼拌黃瓜很好吃/不好吃。

or

Q: 你吃過涼拌黃瓜嗎？

A: 我沒吃過。

Q: 你想吃嗎？

A: 我想吃/我不想吃。

1

_____

_____

2

_____

_____

3

_____

_____

4

_____

_____

5

_____

_____

D Based on the images below, form questions-and-answers about the locations of the person and the items relative to the table. PRESENTATIONAL

1

Q: _____

A: _____

2

Q: _____

A: _____

3

Q: _____

A: _____

4

Q: _____

A: _____

E Locate the buildings based on this map, following the example below. **PRESENTATIONAL**

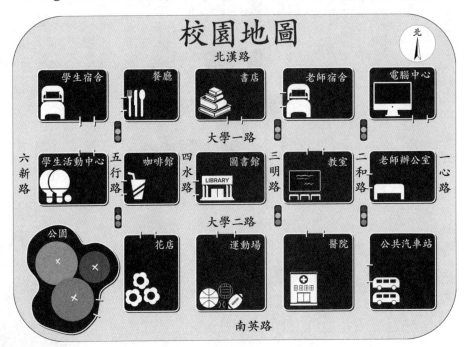

Q: 書店在哪兒？

A: 書店在餐廳的東邊。/書店在老師宿舍的西邊。/書店在餐廳和老師宿舍的中間⋯⋯

1
_____

2
_____

3
_____

F Answer the question based on the map in (E). **INTERPERSONAL**

請問，從公園到電腦中心怎麼走？

_____
_____
_____

Translate these sentences into Chinese. **PRESENTATIONAL**

1 **Student A:** Have you found your red shoes?

_____

   Student B: No, I haven't.

_____

   Student A: I heard your red shoes were expensive. Five hundred dollars?

_____

   Student B: Not that expensive.

_____

2 **Student A:** Have you finished the letter to your mother?

_____

   Student B: No, I haven't finished it. I haven't even started yet.

_____

   Student A: Hurry up, her birthday is coming.

_____

   Student B: OK, I'll do it after I finish drinking this cup of coffee.

_____

3 **Student A:** Have you been to Chinatown?

_____

   Student B: No, never. Where is it?

_____

   Student A: It's not far from here. After the second traffic light, make a right turn, and you'll be there. Would you like to go?

_____

   Student B: OK, let's go now!

_____

4 Student A: I am going to order a hot-and-sour soup today. What would you like to order?

_____

Student B: I've had their hot-and-sour soup before. It is a bit sour and a bit spicy. Quite delicious. But I've never had dumplings here. I am going to order some dumplings.

_____

_____

_____

 H Write a story based on the four images below. Make sure that your story has a beginning, middle, and end, and that the transition from one image to the next is smooth and logical. **PRESENTATIONAL**

1

2

3

4

_____

_____

_____

_____

生日晚會
Birthday Party

 Check off the following items as you learn them.

Useful Expressions

[ ] Here's your birthday gift.

[ ] I'll come pick you up.

[ ] I'll bring some beverages.

[ ] I'm flattered.

[ ] I was born in the year of the _____ (your Chinese zodiac sign).

Cultural Norms

[ ] Chinese zodiac

[ ] Karaoke

[ ] Gift giving

[ ] Party etiquette

As you progress through the lesson, note other useful expressions and cultural norms you would like to learn.

_____

_____

_____

Dialogue 1: Let's Go to a Party!

Audio

Listening Comprehension

A Listen to the Textbook Dialogue 1 audio, then circle the most appropriate choice. INTERPRETIVE

1 **Whose birthday is it?**

   a   Gao Wenzhong's cousin's

   b   Gao Wenzhong's

   c   Gao Xiaoyin's

   d   Gao Xiaoyin's boyfriend's

2 **What won't the host of the party receive from Wang Peng and Li You?**

   a   flowers

   b   fruit

   c   beverages

   d   balloons

3 **What won't the host and guests do at the party?**

   a   sing

   b   dance

   c   watch TV

   d   eat

4 **Who isn't coming to the party?**

   a   Gao Xiaoyin's boyfriend

   b   Gao Xiaoyin's classmate

   c   Gao Xiaoyin's cousin

   d   Gao Xiaoyin's parents

B Listen to the Workbook Narrative audio, then match each item with the person who purchased it. INTERPRETIVE

1   a

2   b

3   c

____ Listen to the Listening Rejoinder audio. After hearing the first speaker, select the best response from the four choices given by the second speaker. Indicate the number of your choice. **INTERPRETIVE**

Pinyin and Tone

A Identify the characters with the same initials (either *j* or *x*) and write them in *pinyin*.

西　姐　些　接　介

1 *j:* _____

2 *x:* _____

B Compare the tones of these characters. Indicate the tones with 1 (first tone), 2 (second tone), 3 (third tone), 4 (fourth tone), or 0 (neutral tone).

1 姐 _____   接 _____
2 飲 _____   音 _____
3 舞 _____   物 _____
4 梨 _____   禮 _____

Speaking

A Answer these questions in Chinese based on Textbook Dialogue 1. **PRESENTATIONAL**

1 Why does Li You call Wang Peng?

2 What will people do at Gao Xiaoyin's place?

3 What will Wang Peng bring?

4 What will Li You bring and why?

5 How will Li You get to Gao Xiaoyin's place and why?

In pairs, role-play inviting a friend to your birthday party. Tell him/her when and where the party is, what people will do, what to bring, and how to get there. Ask your friend if he/she needs a ride. **INTERPERSONAL**

C Tell your classmates about your favorite birthday party, including when and where the party was, what people did, and the reasons it was your favorite. **PRESENTATIONAL**

Reading Comprehension

A If you combine the *rè* in *tiānqi rè* with the *yǐn* in *yǐnliào*, you have *rèyǐn*, as seen in exercise 1 below. Can you guess what the word *rèyǐn* means? Write the characters, *pinyin*, and English equivalent of each new word formed in this way. Consult a dictionary if necessary. **INTERPRETIVE**

1 "天氣熱"的"熱"+"飲料"的"飲"

→ 熱+飲 → _____ _____

2 "天氣冷"的"冷"+"飲料"的"飲"

→ 冷+飲 → _____ _____

3 "英國"的"國"+"一把花"的"花"

→ 國+花 → _____ _____

4 "門"+"路口"的"口"

→ 門+口 → _____ _____

5 "一把花"的"花"+"汽車"的"車"

→ 花+車 → _____ _____

　　昨天是小常二十歲生日，晚上我們在他的宿舍給他過生日。小常的女朋友帶了水果、飲料，還有很多別的好吃的東西。大家一邊吃東西、一邊聊天兒、一邊玩，晚上十二點才回家。因為我昨天回家太晚，所以今天的考試考得糟糕極了。

1 ＿＿＿ Little Chang turned nineteen last year.
2 ＿＿＿ Little Chang's girlfriend prepared snacks, fruit, and drinks for the party.
3 ＿＿＿ Everyone danced and had a great time last night.
4 ＿＿＿ The narrator didn't go to bed until after midnight.
5 ＿＿＿ The narrator did well on today's test.

C Read this dialogue, then mark the statements true or false. **INTERPRETIVE**

（在李友的生日舞會上……）

李友：小藍，喝點兒飲料或者吃點兒水果吧。

小藍：謝謝，我喝茶吧。李友，你看，張英正在跳舞呢。她穿的就是上個週末跟你一起買的那件襯衫，真漂亮。

李友：不對，她跟我一起買的那件是黃的。這件是白的，是你送給她的。你怎麼忘了？

小藍：是啊，我怎麼忘了呢？現在我知道我為什麼這麼喜歡這件襯衫了。

1 ____ Little Lan likes tea better than soda.

2 ____ Li You went shopping with Zhang Ying last weekend.

3 ____ Zhang Ying is wearing a yellow blouse for the party.

4 ____ Zhang Ying bought a white blouse last weekend.

5 ____ Little Lan forgot to give Zhang Ying a present.

D Review this multi-course menu, then answer the following questions. **INTERPRETIVE**

1 Does the meal come with fruit and beverages? How do you know?

_____

2 What do 涼菜 and 熱菜 mean?

_____

A套

涼菜：鮮椒口水雞

　　　熱拌時蔬

　　　五香牛肉

　　　糯米藕夾

　　　蒜泥白肉

　　　鄉巴佬豆干

熱菜：鮮椒美極蝦

　　　香酥樟茶鴨

　　　宮保帶子

　　　水煮鯰魚

　　　剁椒粉絲扇貝

　　　澆汁牛柳

　　　豆瓣肘子

　　　欖菜季豆雞掌脆

　　　草菇扒菜膽

　　　竹筍燉老雞

小吃：雞汁鍋貼

　　　醪糟湯圓

　　　水果拼盤

　　　自製飲料兩扎

A Write the radical 食 in the character 飲 and two characters with the same radical, then provide each character's *pinyin* and meaning in English (write the common radical in 1).

1

2  _____ _____

3  _____ _____

B Answer these questions based on your own preferences. **PRESENTATIONAL**

1 你愛吃什麼水果？

_____

2 你愛喝什麼飲料？

_____

3 你愛吃什麼中國菜？

_____

C Based on the images, form questions-and-answers about what people are doing. Use （正在）…呢 where appropriate, following the example below. **PRESENTATIONAL**

Q: 她（正在）做什麼呢？
A: 她（正在）跳舞呢。

1

Q: _____

A: _____

2

Q: _____

A: _____

3

Q: _____

A: _____

D You are planning a party and need to tell people what to bring. Make your requests based on the images, following the example below. **PRESENTATIONAL**

王朋，請你帶蛋糕 *(dàngāo)*。

1

_____

2

_____

3

_____

E Little Fei is an effusive guy. This comes across in the enthusiastic way he describes things. Write down what he would be likely to say about the following using 極了 to indicate a superlative degree, and be sure to use a different adjective for each sentence. Follow the example below.

PRESENTATIONAL

我住的地方好極了。

1 the car he drives

_____

2 the computer he uses

_____

3 the characters he writes

_____

4 the friends he knows

_____

1 **Student A:** What kind of fruit do you like? Watermelons, pears, or apples?

_____

Student B: I love eating watermelon in the summer and apples in the fall.

_____

2 **Student A:** What are you doing?

_____

Student B: I'm watching TV.

_____

Student A: Gao Wenzhong is having a dance party. Do you feel like going?

_____

Student B: Sure, but his place is very far from my house. Can you come pick me up?

_____

Student A: No problem.

_____

Student B: Thanks. I'll wait for you downstairs at 7:30.

_____

Dialogue 2: Birthday Bash

Audio

Listening Comprehension

A Listen to the Textbook Dialogue 2 audio, then circle the most appropriate choice. INTERPRETIVE

1 Who greets Wang Peng and Li You at the door?

   a Gao Wenzhong

   b Gao Wenzhong's cousin

   c Gao Xiaoyin

   d Bai Ying'ai

2 Who hasn't arrived yet?

   a Wang Hong

   b Helen

   c Tom

   d Bai Ying'ai

3 Who is Tom?

   a Helen's dog

   b Helen's son

   c Helen's boyfriend

   d Helen's cousin

4 Helen speaks Chinese very well because

   a she is Chinese.

   b she was a Chinese teacher.

   c she studied Chinese in summer school.

   d she has a lot of Chinese friends.

B Listen to the Workbook Dialogue audio, then circle the most appropriate choice. INTERPRETIVE

1 The female speaker is the male speaker's

   a mother.

   b sister.

   c girlfriend.

   d cousin.

2 A book wouldn't be a good gift because

   a the speaker's father doesn't have time to read.

   b the speaker's father doesn't like to read.

   c the speaker's father can't read.

   d the speaker's father has too many books already.

3 Coffee wouldn't be a good gift because

a the speaker's father doesn't like coffee.

b the speaker's father has decided to give up caffeine.

c the speaker's father has stopped drinking coffee on his doctor's orders.

d the speaker's father is very picky about coffee.

4 A shirt wouldn't be a good gift because

a the speaker's father doesn't like people buying clothes for him.

b the speaker's father doesn't wear dress shirts.

c the speaker's father doesn't need another shirt.

d it's impossible to find shirts that fit the speaker's father.

5 What would the father like to have on his birthday?

a an outing to the movies

b Chinese food

c time with his children

d time by himself

C Listen to the Workbook Narrative audio, then answer these questions in English based on the speaker's message to her dog-sitter. **INTERPRETIVE**

1 Does the speaker already know the dog-sitter? How do you know?

_____

2 What specific instructions does the speaker give to the dog-sitter? List them in detail.

_____

_____

3 If you were the dog-sitter, would you have any questions for the owner? Ask at least one.

_____

4 Has the dog-sitter ever met the dog? How do you know?

_____

5 Would you dog-sit for the speaker if you were asked? Why or why not?

_____

D _____ Listen to the Listening Rejoinder audio. After hearing the first speaker, select the best response from the four choices given by the second speaker. Indicate the number of your choice. **INTERPRETIVE**

A Identify the characters with the same initials (either *zh* or *z*) and write them in *pinyin*.

鐘　長　最　重　嘴

1 *zh:* _____

2 *z:* _____

B Compare the tones of these characters. Indicate the tones with 1 (first tone), 2 (second tone), 3 (third tone), 4 (fourth tone), or 0 (neutral tone).

1 嘴 _____ 最 _____   **3** 班 _____ 拌 _____

2 聰 _____ 從 _____   **4** 屬 _____ 舒 _____

Speaking

A Answer these questions in Chinese based on Textbook Dialogue 2. PRESENTATIONAL

1 What does Gao Xiaoyin say when she receives birthday presents from Li You and Wang Peng?

2 How much time does Wang Hong spend practicing English every day?

3 Who is Tom?

4 Where did Helen study Chinese?

5 What does Tom look like?

B In pairs, have a conversation about daily activities. Ask each other how much time you ordinarily spend on eating dinner, doing homework, and sleeping every day. INTERPERSONAL

C In pairs, ask each other what year you were born, where you were born, and what your Chinese zodiac sign is. INTERPERSONAL

D Present a photo of someone famous, a family member, or a friend, and describe to your classmates what the person looks like. PRESENTATIONAL

A If you combine the *yǎn* in *yǎnjing* with the *qiú* in *dǎ qiú*, you have *yǎnqiú*, as seen in exercise 1 below. Can you guess what the word *yǎnqiú* means? Complete this section by providing the characters, *pinyin*, and English equivalent of each new word formed in this way. Consult a dictionary if necessary. INTERPRETIVE

1 "眼睛"的"眼"+"打球"的"球"

→ 眼＋球 → ＿＿＿＿＿＿ ＿＿＿＿＿＿

2 "鼻子"的"鼻"+"發音"的"音"

→ 鼻＋音 → ＿＿＿＿ ＿＿＿＿ ＿＿＿＿

3 "蛋糕"的"蛋"+"白色"的"白"

→ 蛋＋白 → ＿＿＿＿＿＿ ＿＿＿＿＿＿

4 "蛋糕"的"蛋"+"黃色"的"黃"

→ 蛋＋黃 → ＿＿＿＿ ＿＿＿＿ ＿＿＿＿

5 "天氣熱"的"熱"+"狗"

→ 熱＋狗 → ＿＿＿＿＿＿ ＿＿＿＿＿＿

B Read this passage, then mark the statements true or false. INTERPRETIVE

張英很喜歡日文班的一個男同學。他們是在一個朋友的生日舞會上認識的，那天他們在一起聊天聊了半個多鐘頭。那個男同學跟張英一樣，是英國人。他的眼睛大大的，鼻子高高的，笑的時候很好看。他又會唱歌又會跳舞。下個星期六學校有個舞會，張英很想請他一起去跳舞，可是不好意思問他。下午下課以後，張英回到宿舍，和她住在一起的李友說："剛才日文班的一個男的給你打電話，請你下個星期六和他一起去跳舞，可是我忘了他姓什麼了。"張英聽了以後，有點兒高興，也有點兒緊張，她希望打電話的就是自己喜歡的那位男同學。

1 ＿＿ 張英喜歡的男孩子是她的朋友的朋友。

2 ＿＿ 那個男孩子學習日文。

3 ＿＿ 張英是英國人，那個男孩子是日本人。

4 ＿＿ 張英想請那個男孩子來她家跳舞。

5 ＿＿ 張英和李友今天上的課是一樣的。

6 ＿＿ 李友知道打電話的那個人是日文班的學
生。

7 ＿＿ 張英知道請她跳舞的那個人就是她喜歡的
那個男孩子。

C Read this dialogue, then mark the statements true or false. **INTERPRETIVE**

（在李友的生日舞會上……）

李友：哎，王朋，你怎麼現在才來？

王朋：對不起，我來晚了。李友，這是
我送給你的生日禮物。

李友：謝謝。

王朋：還有一個禮物。

李友：哎，這是我忘在圖書館的中文書！太好了！你是什麼時候找到的？

王朋：剛找到的。

李友：你是怎麼找到的？

王朋：我有一個朋友，在圖書館工作。他幫我找，我們一起找了兩個多鐘頭才找到。

李友：在哪兒找到的？

王朋：在日文書那邊。圖書館的人不認識中文，他們覺得中文跟日文一樣。你在書上寫的中文名字，他們以為是日文。

李友：王朋，你真好。

1 ＿＿＿ Li You was anxiously awaiting Wang Peng's arrival.

2 ＿＿＿ Wang Peng spent at least two hours in the library today.

3 ＿＿＿ Wang Peng spent a lot of money on his second birthday gift for Li You.

4 ＿＿＿ Wang Peng had told Li You that he would look for her lost book.

D Based on the dialogue in (C), circle the most appropriate choice. **INTERPRETIVE**

1 Why did Wang Peng look for the book today?
  a He wanted to make Li You happy on her birthday.
  b He knew his librarian friend was working today.
  c He wanted to save money on a birthday gift.

2 Why didn't the librarians find the book earlier?

    a Li You didn't write her name on it like she said she had.

    b They couldn't tell written Chinese from written Japanese.

    c They knew that Wang Peng would eventually find it.

E Read this passage, then draw a picture based on what it says and answer the questions in English.
INTERPRETIVE

這是我的狗，他的毛 *(máo)* **(hair, fur)** 是白色的，我叫他小白。因為我屬狗，所以我爸爸媽媽送小白給我做生日禮物。他長得很可愛，臉大大的，嘴小小的，鼻子不高。我常常帶他到公園去玩。他跟我一樣，也喜歡吃肉、喝飲料、不喜歡運動，每天晚上也睡九個鐘頭的覺。你看，這是小白的照片，他正在笑呢！

1 What's the dog's name? Who gave him that name, and why?

2 Why did the narrator's parents give her a dog as a birthday gift?

3 What does the passage tell you about the narrator?

_____

```
Writing and Grammar
```

A   You have just learned the word 聰明 (clever, intelligent). Write down a second word that starts with a character sharing the same pronunciation as the last character in 聰明, then write down a third word with a character sharing the same pronunciation as the last character in the second word, and so on. See how many words you can write down to form a "dragon of words."

_____

_____

B   Form a character by fitting the given components together as indicated, following the example below. Then provide a word or phrase in which that character appears.

左邊一個"女"，右邊一個"子"是"好久不見"的
"好"。

1 左邊一個"女"，右邊一個"且"是 _____
    的 _____。

2 左邊一個"糸"，右邊一個"工"是 _____
    的 _____。

3 上邊一個"日"，下邊一個"者"是 ＿＿＿＿＿＿ 的 ＿＿＿＿ 。

4 左邊一個"工"，右邊一個"力"是 ＿＿＿＿＿＿ 的 ＿＿＿＿ 。

5 左邊一個"目"，右邊一個"青"是 ＿＿＿＿＿＿ 的 ＿＿＿＿ 。

C | Look at the apples on the flyer. Which could be an American Granny Smith?

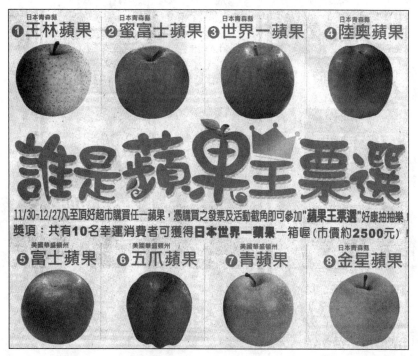

D | Your friend is studying fashion marketing and would like to interview you for an assignment. Answer the following questions based on what you are wearing today. INTERPERSONAL

1 Q: 你的衣服是什麼時候買的？

A: ＿＿＿＿＿＿＿＿＿＿＿＿＿＿＿＿＿＿＿

2 Q: 你的衣服是在哪兒買的？

A: ＿＿＿＿＿＿＿＿＿＿＿＿＿＿＿＿＿＿＿

3 你的衣服是誰買的？

_____

4 你的衣服是花多少錢買的？

_____

E Answer these questions using the "subject + verb + (object + verb) + (了) + duration of time" or "subject + verb + (了) + duration of time + (的) + object" structure according to your own circumstances. **INTERPERSONAL**

1 Q: 你平常每天做功課做多長時間？

A: _____

Q: 昨天呢？

A: _____

2 Q: 你平常吃晚飯吃多長時間？

A: _____

Q: 昨天呢？

A: _____

3 Q: 你平常洗澡洗多長時間？

A: _____

Q: 昨天呢？

A: _____

F Describe this dog. Include as many details as you can. **PRESENTATIONAL**

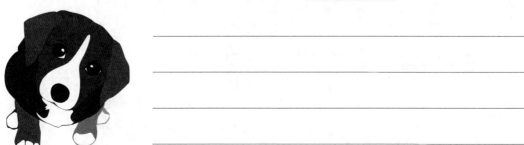

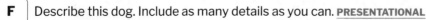

G Describe what your ideal boyfriend/girlfriend would look like. PRESENTATIONAL

_____

_____

_____

_____

H Translate these sentences into Chinese. PRESENTATIONAL

1 **Student A:** Little Li is a good student. He is both smart and hardworking.

_____

Student B: I heard he does homework for four hours every night.

_____

Student A: But he likes to exercise, too. We exercised for an hour yesterday afternoon at the student center.

_____

_____

Student B: Really? He is quite busy.

_____

2 **Student A:** Who's that guy ice-skating?

_____

Student B: That's my boyfriend, Tom.

_____

Student A: He's quite handsome. Is he older or younger than you?

_____

Student B: He's the same age as I am. We were both born in 2000.

_____

Student A: Where did you meet?

_____

Student B: We met at school.

_____

I You are planning a birthday party for your best friend. Write up a plan for the guest of honor to review. The plan needs to include information such as who you are inviting, where the party will take place, what people can bring to the party, what activities there will be, how long each activity will last, and what gifts your friend might wish to receive. Some of the party guests may need a ride to the party; include suggestions for their transportation plans. PRESENTATIONAL

_____

_____

_____

_____

J Write a story in Chinese based on the four images below. Make sure that your story has a beginning, middle, and end, and that the transition from one image to the next is smooth and logical. PRESENTATIONAL

1

2

3

4

_____

_____

_____

_____

看病
Seeing a Doctor

 Check off the following items as you learn them.

Useful Expressions

[ ] My stomach is killing me!

[ ] I caught a cold.

[ ] I'm allergic to _____.

[ ] Do I need to take any injections?

[ ] Take this medicine _____ (#) times a day, _____ (#) pills at a time.

Cultural Norms

[ ] Chinese medicine

[ ] Seeing the doctor

[ ] Medical care

[ ] Alternative medical treatments

As you progress through the lesson, note other useful expressions and cultural norms you would like to learn.

_____

_____

_____

Dialogue 1: My Stomach Is Killing Me!

Audio

Listening Comprehension

A Listen to the Textbook Dialogue 1 audio, then circle the most appropriate choice. **INTERPRETIVE**

1 **When did Gao Wenzhong start feeling under the weather?**

   a   last week

   b   five days ago

   c   yesterday morning

   d   last night

2 **Why does Gao Wenzhong have a stomachache?**

   a   He had too much ice.

   b   He has an ulcer.

   c   He ate some spoiled food.

   d   He drank polluted water.

3 **How much medication does Gao Wenzhong need to take, and how often?**

   a   three pills twice a day

   b   two pills three times a day

   c   one pill three times a day

   d   two pills twice a day

4 **The doctor recommends that Gao Wenzhong**

   a   abstain from food for twenty-four hours.

   b   drink nothing but water for twenty-four hours.

   c   rest for twenty-four hours.

   d   come back to the clinic in twenty-four hours.

B Listen to the Workbook Narrative audio, and then select the appropriate answer to each question. **INTERPRETIVE**

1 **Why is the dog named Little Bai?**

   a   It is white.

   b   The speaker's family name is Bai.

   c   The doctor's last name is White.

   d   It loves white toys.

2 **What does the speaker take Little Bai to see the doctor annually for?**

   a   a physical check up

   b   an immunization injection

   c   both a and b

   d   neither a nor b

3 According to the doctor, what could result from Little Bai eating human food?

  a He could be healthier than other dogs.

  b He could become bigger than other dogs.

  c He could have to go to the bathroom more often.

  d He could be more liable to get sick.

4 What is the doctor's advice to the speaker?

  a Walk Little Bai more often.

  b Don't feed Little Bai human food.

  c Take Little Bai to the bathroom more often.

  d Take Little Bai to see the doctor twice a year.

C _____ Listen to the Listening Rejoinder audio. After hearing the first speaker, select the best response from the four choices given by the second speaker. Indicate the number of your choice. **INTERPRETIVE**

Pinyin and Tone

A Identify the characters with the same finals (either *an* or *ian*) and write them in *pinyin*.

片 蛋 臉 檢 辦

1 *an:* _____

2 *ian:* _____

B Compare the tones of these characters. Indicate the tones with 1 (first tone), 2 (second tone), 3 (third tone), 4 (fourth tone), or 0 (neutral tone).

1 夜 _____ 也 _____   **3** 約 _____ 越 _____

2 病 _____ 冰 _____   **4** 院 _____ 圓 _____

Speaking

A Answer these questions in Chinese based on Textbook Dialogue 1. **PRESENTATIONAL**

1 Why does Gao Wenzhong go to the doctor?

2 How did his symptoms start?

3　What does the doctor say about the cause of his illness?

4　What are the instructions on his prescription?

5　What does the doctor suggest that Gao Wenzhong should do in addition to taking the medication?

B　In pairs, role-play a conversation between a doctor and a patient. The patient describes his/her symptoms and asks the doctor about the treatment. The doctor responds and gives instructions based on the label below. **INTERPERSONAL**

內服藥

＿＿＿＿＿＿＿先生

＿＿＿＿＿＿＿女士

每日 _4_ 次，每次 _1_ 片　　飯後

每 _6_ 小時服用一次

Reading Comprehension

A　If you combine the *Zhōng* in *Zhōngguó* with the *yī* in *yīshēng*, you have *Zhōngyī*, as seen in exercise 1 below. Can you guess what the word *Zhōngyī* means? Complete this section by writing the characters, *pinyin*, and English equivalent of each new word formed in this way. Consult a dictionary if necessary. **INTERPRETIVE**

1　"中國"的"中"＋"醫生"的"醫"

→ 中＋醫 → ＿＿＿＿＿　＿＿＿＿＿　＿＿＿＿＿

2　"東南西北"的"西"＋"醫生"的"醫"

→ 西＋醫 → ＿＿＿＿＿　＿＿＿＿＿　＿＿＿＿＿

3　"公共汽車"的"公"＋"廁所"的"廁"

→ 公＋廁 → ＿＿＿＿＿　＿＿＿＿＿　＿＿＿＿＿

4 "寫信"的"信"＋"冰箱"的"箱"

→ 信＋箱 → _____ _____ _____

5 "吃藥"的"藥"＋"檢查"的"檢"

→ 藥＋檢 → _____ _____ _____

B Read this passage, then mark the statements true or false. **INTERPRETIVE**

因為今天要考試，小黃昨天晚上把功課做完以後就開始看書，今天早上四點才睡覺，六點就起床了。一起床他就覺得頭有一點兒疼。考完試以後，小黃的頭更疼了，就去看病。醫生說小黃沒什麼問題，只是睡覺不夠，今天晚上多睡一點就好了。醫生沒有給他打針，也沒給他藥吃。

1 _____ 小黃昨天晚上先做功課，然後看書。

2 _____ 因為小黃考試考得不好，所以他頭疼。

3 _____ 考試以後，小黃的頭比起床的時候更疼了。

4 _____ 醫生覺得小黃的病很重。

5 _____ 醫生告訴小黃今天晚上得多睡覺。

6 _____ 醫生覺得小黃不用打針，也不用吃藥。

C Read this passage, then mark the statements true or false. **INTERPRETIVE**

小錢以前住在學生宿舍，每天在學生餐廳吃飯。餐廳的菜很便宜，可是不好吃，小錢常常吃很少一點東西就不想再吃了。小錢的媽媽知道了，就說，"回家來住吧。"這個學期小錢住在家裡，每天都吃媽媽做的菜，覺得好吃極了。小錢家離學校很遠，她每天早上很早就得起床，然後坐地鐵去上課。因為她睡覺睡得不夠，眼睛常常是紅紅的，有點兒不舒服。可是小錢還是覺得住在家裡比住在學生宿舍好。

1 ＿＿ Little Qian has been living at home for a year.

2 ＿＿ When she lived on campus, Little Qian had to spend a lot of money on food.

3 ＿＿ Little Qian's mom is a good cook.

4 ＿＿ Little Qian's eyes are often red because of some kind of allergy.

5 ＿＿ We can assume that Little Qian will not move back to the dorm soon.

D Read this passage, then mark the statements true or false. **INTERPRETIVE**

李友星期四晚上請王紅教她做了一盤家常豆腐，沒吃完，就把沒吃完的豆腐放在冰箱裡了。星期五李友吃早飯的時候，吃了幾口豆腐，上課的時候肚子就疼起來了。李友一下課就去看病，醫生檢查了一下，說是吃壞肚子了。李友不懂那盤豆腐在冰箱裡只放了八、九個小時，怎麼會把肚子吃壞了呢？她打電話請王朋來幫她看看冰箱，王朋檢查了以後說："冰箱壞了。"

1 ____ Li You cooked a tofu dish and invited Wang Hong to dinner.

2 ____ The tofu dish was the cause of Li You's stomachache.

3 ____ When Li You went to the doctor, it took the doctor a long time to diagnose the problem.

4 ____ Until she saw the doctor, Li You had taken for granted that her refrigerator was functioning properly.

5 ____ Li You asked Wang Peng to help her look for a new refrigerator.

E This is an instruction label on a prescription drug bottle. Explain in Chinese what you think the character 服 and the instructions 空肚服 and 睡前服 mean.

INTERPRETIVE

1 _____

2 _____

  _____

3 _____

  _____

姓 名
日 期

每日服 .... 次，每次服 .... 粒
每隔 .... 小時服 1 次

☐ 空 肚 服   ☐ 飽 肚 服
☐ 早 上 服   ☐ 睡 前 服
☐ 咬 碎 服   ☐ 含 口 服
☐ 發 燒 服   ☐ 需 要 時 服
☐ 服藥後可能會有睡意、忌駕駛、忌飲酒

藥 名

Writing and Grammar

A Write the radical in the character 針 and three more characters with the same radical. Then compound each character with another one to form a word or phrase, and provide their meanings in English (write the radical in 1).

1 ⊞

2 ⊞ _____ _____

3

4 _____ _____

B Form questions-and-answers based on the images provided, following the example below.

Q: 醫生做什麼呢？

A: 醫生給病人看病呢。

1

Q: _____

A: _____

2

Q: _____

A: _____

3

Q: _____

A: _____

C Answer these questions according to your own circumstances. INTERPERSONAL

1 Q: 你每個星期上幾次中文課？

A: _____

2 Q: 你每個星期工作幾次？

A: _____

3 Q: 你每個星期運動幾次？

A: _____

4 Q: 你每個月洗幾次衣服？

A: _____

5 Q: 你昨天喝了幾次水？

A: _____

D Your younger brother is coming to stay with you for a few weeks. Based on the images, use 把 to write down instructions on where he should place his things, following the example below.

PRESENTATIONAL

 　把西瓜放在冰箱裡。

1

_____

2

_____

3

_____

4

_____

5

_____

E What does your teacher often say to the class? Translate these sentences into Chinese, using 把. Follow the example below. **PRESENTATIONAL**

Please hand in your homework.

請把功課給我。

1 Please finish your homework.

_____

2 Please finish listening to the audio.

_____

3 Please write the characters correctly.

_____

F Translate these sentences into Chinese. **PRESENTATIONAL**

1 **Student A:** Where is the watermelon I bought?

_____

   Student B: I put it in the refrigerator.

_____

2 **Student A:** I drank three glasses of water before bed last night, and I went to the bathroom twice late last night.

_____

   Student B: You'd better not drink any water before bed.

_____

3 The teacher asked us to listen to the audio recording ten times every day. But I often listen to it three times. Last night, I only listened once. I hope the teacher won't ask me to read the text aloud today. I will definitely do a very bad job.

_____

_____

_____

_____

Dialogue 2: Allergies

Audio

Listening Comprehension

A Listen to the Textbook Dialogue 2 audio, then circle the appropriate choice. **INTERPRETIVE**

1 Why are Wang Peng's eyes red?

   a   They are infected.

   b   He is suffering from allergies.

   c   He has been crying.

   d   He is wearing contact lenses.

2 Why has Wang Peng been self-medicating?

   a   He doesn't have health insurance.

   b   He is too busy to see a doctor.

   c   He has the right medicine.

   d   He knows a lot about medicine.

3 Li You thinks that Wang Peng should

   a   take being sick more seriously.

   b   be more careful with his money.

   c   not be too reliant on pills.

   d   not worry about his health excessively.

4 Li You offers to

   a   buy some new medicine for Wang Peng.

   b   lend Wang Peng some money for better health insurance.

   c   go to the doctor's office with Wang Peng.

   d   call a doctor friend for advice.

B Listen to the Workbook Narrative audio, then mark these statements true or false. **INTERPRETIVE**

1 _____ The message was left by the caller on her brother's answering machine.

2 _____ The caller's mother called today.

3 _____ The mother doesn't know that her son is suffering from allergies.

4 _____ The caller told her mother that her brother would seek treatment.

5 _____ The caller wants her brother to call their mother.

6 _____ The caller would like to see a Chinese film tomorrow.

C _____ Listen to the Listening Rejoinder audio. After hearing the first speaker, select the best response from the four choices given by the second speaker. Indicate the number of your choice. **INTERPRETIVE**

A Identify the characters with the same initials (either *j* or *zh*) and write them in *pinyin*.

健　針　住　檢　種

1 *j:* _____

2 *zh:* _____

B Compare the tones of these characters. Indicate the tones with 1 (first tone), 2 (second tone), 3 (third tone), 4 (fourth tone), or 0 (neutral tone).

1 毛 _____ 冒 _____　　3 健 _____ 檢 _____

2 懶 _____ 藍 _____　　4 癢 _____ 樣 _____

Speaking

A Answer these questions in Chinese based on Textbook Dialogue 2. PRESENTATIONAL

1 What are Wang Peng's symptoms?

2 What does Li You think Wang Peng's problem is?

3 Where did Wang Peng get his medication?

4 Why hasn't Wang Peng seen a doctor?

5 What does Wang Peng plan to do about his illness?

B In pairs, discuss what you and your partner do when you have a cold. Do you see a doctor, take medicine, rest, or stay home from school or work? INTERPERSONAL

C In pairs, pretend that you are feeling ill, but you don't feel like seeing the doctor. Describe your symptoms and explain why you don't want to go to the doctor. Your partner will try his/her best to change your mind. INTERPERSONAL

A If you combine the *bìng* in *shēng bìng* with the *chuáng* in *qǐ chuáng*, you have *bìngchuáng*, as seen in exercise 1 below. Can you guess what the word *bìngchuáng* means? Complete this section by writing the characters, *pinyin*, and English equivalent of each new word formed in this way. Consult a dictionary if necessary. INTERPRETIVE

1 "生病"的"病"＋"起床"的"床"

→ 病＋床 → _____ _____ _____

2 "生病"的"病"＋"寒假"的"假"

→ 病＋假 → _____ _____ _____

3 "身體"的"身"＋"高"

→ 身＋高 → _____ _____ _____

4 "身體"的"體"＋"檢查"的"檢"

→ 體＋檢 → _____ _____ _____

5 "身體"的"體"＋"重"

→ 體＋重 → _____ _____ _____

B Read this dialogue, then mark the statements true or false. INTERPRETIVE

醫生：你哪兒不舒服？

病人：醫生，我肚子疼死了。

醫生：我給你檢查一下。你昨天吃什麼
東西了？

病人：我昨天晚上吃了一盤糖醋魚和幾個餃子。

醫生：我知道了，一定是那盤糖醋魚有問題。你得趕快吃藥，要不然你的肚子會越來越疼。你去的那個飯館一定很便宜，對不對？你以後出去吃飯，一定要去貴的飯館。雖然多付一點錢，可是吃了不會生病。

病人：您說得對，那家飯館很便宜，可是我覺得那盤魚真的很好吃，不會有問題。

醫生：你是在哪個飯館吃的？

病人：在我們學校南邊的那家小飯館。

醫生：是嗎？……哎，糟糕了！

病人：醫生，您怎麼了？

醫生：我的肚子也疼起來了，昨天晚上我也是在那家飯館吃的晚飯。

1 ____ The patient and the doctor meet in a restaurant.

2 ____ The patient has a stomachache.

3 ____ Neither the doctor nor the patient had dinner at home yesterday.

4 ____ The doctor urges the patient to take medicine as soon as possible.

5 ____ The doctor always dines at expensive restaurants.

C Based on the dialogue in (B), circle the most appropriate choice. **INTERPRETIVE**

1 **What is the doctor's logic as he tries to diagnose the patient's problem?**

   a If the food was the problem, the restaurant must have been cheap.

   b If the patient got a stomachache, he must have eaten spoiled fish.

   c If a restaurant is cheap, it must serve cheap fish dishes.

2 **What is the doctor's advice to the patient about dining out?**

   a Go to more expensive restaurants where the food is tastier.

   b Go to more reputable restaurants where the food is more expensive.

   c Go to more expensive restaurants where the food is safer.

3 **What can we say about the doctor?**

   a He himself follows the advice he gives to his patient.

   b He himself does not follow the advice he gives to his patient.

   c He doesn't eat at cheap restaurants himself.

D Read this passage, then mark the statements true or false. **INTERPRETIVE**

　　小高這幾天一直不舒服。上個週末他頭疼，醫生給了他一些藥，他吃了兩次就好了。可是星期一小高覺得鼻子很癢，眼睛紅紅的。醫生說他一定是對什麼過敏了。醫生給了他一種藥，可是小高吃了三天，一點兒用也沒有。今天上午小高又去看病，想請醫生給點兒別的藥試試。醫生請他把他吃的藥拿出來看看，才知道小高這幾天吃的不是醫生給的過敏藥，是頭疼藥！

1 ＿＿＿ 小高上個週末和這個星期都不太舒服。

2 ＿＿＿ 小高吃了頭疼藥，頭很快就不疼了。

3 ＿＿＿ 上個星期天小高把頭疼藥都吃完了。

4 _____ 醫生說，小高對頭疼藥過敏，所以眼睛紅紅的。

5 _____ 星期三小高的眼睛不紅了，鼻子也不癢了。

6 _____ 小高今天上午又去看醫生，因為他覺得醫生給他的過敏藥沒有用。

7 _____ 因為小高吃錯藥了，所以他的病還沒好。

E Read this passage, then mark the statements true or false. INTERPRETIVE

　　李友的朋友小錢很喜歡學校醫院的一位男醫生。小錢身體很健康，可是為了去看那位醫生，就說自己鼻子癢，眼睛疼，一定是對什麼過敏了。李友一邊笑一邊說："你平常不過敏，怎麼一看到那位長得很帥的男醫生眼睛就疼起來，鼻子就癢起來了？你一定是對那位醫生過敏了。"

1 _____ Little Qian first met the doctor when she went to the hospital for her allergies.

2 _____ According to Li You, Little Qian has suffered from allergies for a long time.

3 _____ According to Li You, allergies are Little Qian's excuse for visiting this particular doctor.

4 _____ Li You knows Little Qian very well.

5 _____ Little Qian's allergy symptoms became worse when she saw the doctor.

6 _____ Li You suggests that Little Qian see a different doctor.

F This is a form for new patients to complete. Fill in as many blanks as you can. Locate the area asking if the patient is allergic to any medications. **INTERPRETIVE**

科　　別：□內□婦□傷□針灸科 □其他　　　病歷號碼＿＿＿＿＿＿＿

初診日期：　年　　月　　日　　□二年以上未至本院看診 □健保□自費

姓　　名		身份證字號		姓別	□男□女
出生日期		電話號碼		職業	
出 生 地		手機號碼		血型	
地　　址					
教育程度	□無　□小學　□國中　□高中　□大學　□大學以上				
婚姻狀況	□未婚　　□已婚　　□離婚　　□寡				
個 人 史	飲食習慣：□素食□辛辣□冷飲□溫熱食品□烤炸食品□外食□無特殊嗜好 過敏：□無 □藥物＿＿＿＿＿＿＿＿＿＿；□食物＿＿＿＿＿＿＿＿ 抽煙：□無 □有　包/天　年。喝酒：□無 □有　瓶/天，　年（酒類＿＿＿）				
家族病史	□糖尿病＿＿ □高血壓＿＿ □心臟病＿＿ □腎臟病＿＿ □異位性皮膚炎＿ □中　風＿＿ □癌　症＿＿ □氣　喘＿＿ □鼻過敏＿＿ □＿＿＿＿				

Writing and Grammar

A Write the radical 心 in the character 感 and three characters with the same radical. Then compound each character with another one to form a word or phrase, and provide their meanings in English (write the radical in 1).

1　[grid box] ＿＿＿＿＿＿＿＿＿＿＿＿

2　[grid box] ＿＿＿＿＿＿＿＿　＿＿＿＿＿＿＿＿

3 _____ _____

4 _____ _____

B Form a character by fitting the given components together as indicated, following the example below. Then provide a word or phrase in which that character appears.

外邊一個"囗"，裡邊一個"口"是"回家"的"回"。

1 左邊一個"月"，右邊一個"土"是 _____ 的 _____ 。

2 外邊一個"疒"，裡邊一個"冬"是 _____ 的 _____ 。

3 左邊一個"金"，右邊一個"十"是 _____ 的 _____ 。

4 左邊一個"亻"，右邊一個"木"是 _____ 的 _____ 。

5 上邊一個"自"，下邊一個"心"是 _____ 的 _____ 。

C In Chinese, list possible symptoms of the following ailments. **PRESENTATIONAL**

1 感冒：

_____

2 過敏：

_____

3 拉 (lā) 肚子 (diarrhea)：

_____

D Based on the images, use 對 to explain what each person is allergic to. Follow the example below.
PRESENTATIONAL

高文中對味精過敏。

1

_____

2

_____

3

_____

4

_____

E Use 越來越 to answer these questions according to your own circumstances. **INTERPERSONAL**

1 Q: 最近越來越冷還是越來越暖和？

A: _____

2 Q: 你的功課越來越多還是越來越少？

A: _____

3 Q: 健康保險越來越貴還是越來越便宜？

A: _____

4 Q: 找工作越來越容易還是越來越難？

A: _____

F Translate these sentences into Chinese. **PRESENTATIONAL**

1 **Student A:** Do you have a fever?

_____

Student B: I do, but I bought some medicine.

_____

Student A: You can't just take any kind of medicine when you have a fever. You'd better see the doctor.

_____

_____

2 **Student A:** Take out the clothes you bought so I can take a look.

_____

Student B: Here they are.

_____

Student A: Why did you buy these clothes?

_____

Student B: Because they fit well, and besides, they were cheap, too.

_____

3 **Student A:** What's the matter with you? Do you have a cold?

_____

Student B: My eyes are itchy. I think I'm allergic to your dog.

_____

Student A: But you've been to my house five or six times . . .

_____

Student B: My eyes are getting itchier and itchier. Please hurry and give me a ride to see the doctor.

_____

Student A: I'll give you a ride if you have health insurance. Otherwise, how about you lie down for a while after taking this medicine that my doctor gave me?

_____

_____

G Write a story in Chinese based on the four images below. Make sure that your story has a beginning, middle, and end, and that the transition from one image to the next is smooth and logical. PRESENTATIONAL

1

2

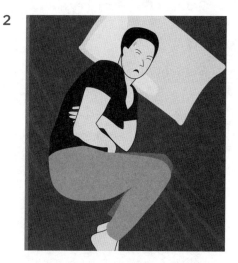

3

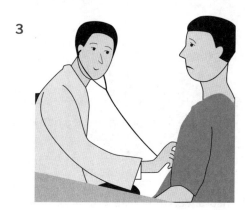

4

每天三次 每次兩片

Bringing It Together (Lessons 11–15)

Pinyin and Tone

A Compare the characters' pronunciation and tones, then write them in *pinyin*.

1	出去	_____	去年	_____
2	下雪	_____	下雨	_____
3	預報	_____	運動	_____
4	肚子	_____	舞會	_____
5	路口	_____	暑期班	_____
6	糖醋魚	_____	紅綠燈	_____
7	牛肉	_____	水果	_____
8	越來越亂	_____	我約你	_____
9	不餓	_____	不渴	_____
10	菜夠了	_____	我屬狗	_____
11	長短	_____	長大	_____
12	覺得	_____	睡覺	_____

A Group these characters according to their radicals.

肚　暖　冷　綠　桌　素　熱　醋
餓　暑　疼　冰　餃　約　糟　病
酸　糕　精　燈　樓　臉　燒　癢
梨　飲

	Radical	Characters
1	_____	_____
2	_____	_____
3	_____	_____
4	_____	_____
5	_____	_____
6	_____	_____
7	_____	_____
8	_____	_____
9	_____	_____
10	_____	_____

Characters

A Circle the common character in each pair of words. Write down the *pinyin* for the character in common, then define its original meaning.

1 預習　　預報　　_____　_____

2 非常　　家常豆腐　_____　_____

3 售貨員　服務員　　_____　_____

4 考試　　面試　　　_____　_____

5 糟糕　　蛋糕　　　_____　_____

6 老師　　師傅　　　_____　_____

7 黃色　　黃瓜　　　_____　_____

8 黃瓜　　西瓜　　　_____　_____

9 運動場　活動中心　_____　_____

10 飛機場　運動場　　_____　_____

11 商店　　書店　　　_____　_____

12 地圖　　圖書館　　_____　_____

13 跳舞　　舞會　　　_____　_____

14 水果　　如果　　　_____　_____

15 功課　　用功　　　_____　_____

16 醫生　　醫院　　　_____　_____

17 冰茶　　冰箱　　　_____　_____

18 發燒　　紅燒牛肉

A Circle the verbs that are VO compounds.

滑冰　　　下雪　　　點菜　　　檢查
看病　　　過敏　　　聽說　　　打針

Communication

A Interview one of your classmates, jot down the information you gather, then present an oral or written report to introduce him/her to the rest of the class.

Food Preferences and Habits

1 你平常晚飯能吃幾碗米飯？吃得下吃不下兩碗？

2 你先吃飯再喝湯還是先喝湯再吃飯？

3 你吃素嗎？

4 你能不能吃辣的？

5 要是你很餓，你想吃什麼？

6 你最愛喝什麼飲料？

7 你最愛吃什麼水果？

8 你做飯的時候放不放味精？

9 你對味精過敏嗎？

10 要是你在飯館點菜，但是你想吃的菜賣完了，你怎麼辦？

11 你常常吃壞肚子嗎？

12 如果肚子疼，你怎麼辦？

Clothing and Style

1 你今天穿的衣服是在哪兒買的？

2 是什麼時候買的？

3 是誰買的？

4 是花多少錢買的？

5 你覺得衣服的大小、顏色、樣子（對你）合適不合適？

Living Situation and Commute

1 你的學校在你住的地方的哪一邊？

2 你的學校離你住的地方遠不遠？

3 你去過學校的學生活動中心嗎？在圖書館的哪一邊？

4 你平常幾點去學校上課？今天呢？今天是幾點去學校上課的？

5 你平常怎麼去學校上課？今天呢？今天是怎麼去學校上課的？

Academics

1 你為什麼上這個學校？

2 你在這個學校學習了多長時間了？

3 你每個星期上幾次中文課？每次上多長
時間？

4 你會用中文發電子郵件嗎？

5 你常常上網用中文跟人聊天兒嗎？

Dream Date

1 你希望你的男／女朋友長得怎麼樣？

2 你希望你的男／女朋友是哪一年生的？
屬什麼？

3 你希望你的男／女朋友比你聰明、比你酷嗎？

4 如果你想約你的男／女朋友出去玩兒，你們會
去什麼地方？

約會
Dating

 Check off the following items as you learn them.

Useful Expressions

[ ] Anyone else going with us?

[ ] It's a deal!

[ ] I cannot remember.

[ ] This weekend won't do.

[ ] My cell phone ran out of battery.

Cultural Norms

[ ] Traditional marriage

[ ] Dates

[ ] Saving face

[ ] Matchmaking corners

As you progress through the lesson, note other useful expressions and cultural norms you would like to learn.

_____

_____

_____

Dialogue 1: Seeing a Movie

Audio

Listening Comprehension

A Listen to the Textbook Dialogue 1 audio, then mark these statements true or false. **INTERPRETIVE**

1 _____ Wang Peng and Li You have known each other for almost six months.

2 _____ There is a showing of a Chinese film at school tonight.

3 _____ Wang Peng had no trouble getting tickets.

4 _____ Li You has seen many Chinese films before.

5 _____ Wang Peng and Li You will be going to the film with friends.

B Listen to the Workbook Dialogue audio, then answer the questions below. **INTERPRETIVE**

1 What does the man offer to do? List four things.

a _____

b _____

c _____

d _____

2 What are the four reasons that the woman gives for not accepting the man's invitations and offers?

a _____

b _____

c _____

d _____

3 What does the woman really want?

_____

4 Does the man get the message?

_____

C ____ Listen to the Listening Rejoinder audio. After hearing the first speaker, select the best response from the four choices given by the second speaker. Indicate the number of your choice. **INTERPRETIVE**

Speaking

A Answer these questions in Chinese based on Textbook Dialogue 1. **PRESENTATIONAL**

   1 How long have Li You and Wang Peng known each other?

   2 How did Li You and Wang Peng become good friends?

   3 What would Wang Peng like to invite Li You to do this weekend?

   4 Was it easy for Wang Peng to get the tickets? Why or why not?

   5 What additional plans have Wang Peng and Li You made for the day of the event?

B In pairs, role-play inviting your partner to the movies this weekend. Decide together which movie you should see and discuss what you could do before and after. **INTERPERSONAL**

C Present to the class how you met your best friend, how long you have known each other, why you like him/her, and what you usually do together. **PRESENTATIONAL**

Pinyin and Tone

A Identify the characters with the same finals (either *in* or *ing*) and write them in *pinyin*.

印　影　興　信　定

   1 *in:* _____

   2 *ing:* _____

B Compare the tones of these characters. Indicate the tones with 1 (first tone), 2 (second tone), 3 (third tone), 4 (fourth tone), or 0 (neutral tone).

   1 印 _____   音 _____   3 費 _____   飛 _____

   2 演 _____   言 _____   4 像 _____   香 _____

Reading Comprehension

A If you combine the *tóng* in *tóng yí ge* with the *bān* in *shǔqí bān*, you have *tóngbān*, as seen in exercise 1 below. Can you guess what the word *tóngbān* means? Write the characters, *pinyin*, and English equivalent of each new word formed in this way. Consult a dictionary if necessary. **INTERPRETIVE**

1 "同一個"的"同"+"暑期班"的"班"

→ 同+班 → _____ _____ _____

2 "手"+"印象"的"印"

→ 手+印 → _____ _____ _____

3 "演電影"的"演"+"服務員"的"員"

→ 演+員 → _____ _____ _____

4 "費力氣"的"費"+"時間"的"時"

→ 費+時 → _____ _____ _____

5 "後天"的"後"+"今年"的"年"

→ 後+年 → _____ _____ _____

B Read this passage, then mark the statements true or false. **INTERPRETIVE**

　　小謝跟小黃認識已經快兩年了，他們是英文班的同學。小黃去過英國，英文說得很好，常常幫小謝練習說英文。小黃做飯做得不太好，週末的時候，小謝常常請小黃到她家去吃飯。小黃對小謝的印象越來越好。小謝覺得小黃又聰明，又用功，對他的印象也很好。上個週末小謝的爸爸媽媽來看她，小謝把小黃介紹給爸媽認識。小謝的爸媽覺得小黃長得不錯，學習也不錯，很喜歡他。

1 ＿＿＿ 小謝的英文老師也是小黃的英文老師。

2 ＿＿＿ 兩年以前小謝不認識小黃。

3 ＿＿＿ 小謝說英文說得比小黃好。

4 ＿＿＿ 週末小謝常常請小黃到飯館去吃飯。

5 ＿＿＿ 小黃覺得小謝是個很好的女孩子。

6 ＿＿＿ 小謝喜歡小黃，但小謝的爸媽覺得他們在一起不合適。

C Read this dialogue, then answer the questions in English. **INTERPRETIVE**

　　高文中對白英愛的印象很好，可是他不知道白英愛對他的印象怎麼樣，所以一直沒有告訴姐姐高小音他喜歡白英愛，朋友們也都不知道。小音問他喜歡什麼樣的女孩子，文中說："眼睛大大的，鼻子高高的，嘴不大也不小。得聰明，會跳舞，還會做飯。"小音覺得要找到這麼好的女孩子，得費很大力氣。文中又說："那個女孩子最好姓白。"小音才知道文中說的一定是白英愛。

1　Why hasn't Gao Wenzhong told his sister how he feels about Bai Ying'ai?

_____

2 Do any of Gao Wenzhong's friends know for sure how Gao Wenzhong feels about Bai Ying'ai? Why or why not?

_____

3 What is Gao Wenzhong's dream partner like?

_____

4 Was Gao Xiaoyin optimistic at first about her brother's chances of meeting his dream partner? Why or why not?

_____

5 Does Gao Xiaoyin now know who Gao Wenzhong's dream partner is? Who is she?

_____

D Review the listing, then answer the following questions. **INTERPRETIVE**

> ❋ 印象電影院
> 週二全天半價：週一至五 12:00前半價
> 上映影片：
> 《危情24小時》 9:00 10:55 12:50
> 14:45 16:40 18:35
> 《功夫熊貓》 9:00 11:50 12:40
> 13:40 15:30 16:20 17:20 19:10
> 20:00 20:30 21:00
> 《精舞門》 10:50 14:30 18:10

1 What's the name of the movie theater? _____

2 How many movies are currently playing at the theater? _____

3 How many showings are there daily for the first movie? _____

4 Can you get half-price tickets for Monday morning showings? _____

Writing and Grammar

A Write the radical 氵 in the character 演 and three more characters with the same radical. Then compound each character with another one to form a word or phrase, and provide their meanings in English (write the radical in 1).

1 [ ] _____

2 [ ] _____ _____

3 [   ] _____ _____

4 [   ] _____ _____

B Answer these questions in Chinese according to your own circumstances. INTERPERSONAL

1 Q: 你去過哪些城市？

A: _____

Q: 你對哪一個城市的印象最糟糕？

A: _____

2 Q: 你去過哪些學校？

A: _____

Q: 你對哪一個學校的印象最好？

A: _____

3 Q: 你看過中國電影嗎？

A: _____

Q: 你對中國電影的印象怎麼樣？

A: _____

C Are the following items available for purchase where you live? Use 得 or 不 where appropriate to write questions-and-answers, following the example below. PRESENTATIONAL

中國音樂

Q: 這個城市買得到買不到中國音樂？

A: 這個城市買得到中國音樂。/
這個城市買不到中國音樂。

1 中文書

Q: _____

A: _____

2 中國地圖

Q: _____

A: _____

3 中國綠茶

Q: _____

A: _____

D Are the following dishes available at your local restaurants? Use 得 or 不 where appropriate to write questions-and-answers, following the example below. **PRESENTATIONAL**

紅燒牛肉

Q: 你住的城市能吃到紅燒牛肉嗎？

A: 我住的城市吃得到紅燒牛肉。/
　 我住的城市吃不到紅燒牛肉。

1 涼拌黃瓜

Q: _____

A: _____

2 糖醋魚

Q: _____

A: _____

3 家常豆腐

Q: _____

A: _____

E You are leaving on a trip tomorrow night and your roommate is double-checking with you whether you can finish the food in your refrigerator before you leave. Use 得 or 不 where appropriate to write questions-and-answers, following the example below. **PRESENTATIONAL**

米飯 ✅

Q: 冰箱裡的米飯，明天吃得完吃不完？

A: （冰箱裡的米飯，明天）吃得完。

1 青菜 ❌

Q: _____

A: _____

2 餃子 ✅

Q: _____

A: _____

3 飲料 ❌

Q: _____

A: _____

4 湯 ✅

Q: _____

A: _____

Translate these sentences into Chinese. **PRESENTATIONAL**

1   **Student A:**   There are six pears on the table. Would you like to eat some?

_____

Student B: I can't eat pears. I'm allergic to them.

_____

Student C: I can eat them. But six pears are too many. I can't eat them all.

_____

2   **Student A:**   I made three hundred dumplings yesterday. It took a lot of effort to get the dumplings ready.

_____

Student B: How many people were making the dumplings?

_____

Student A: Only me, one person.

_____

3   **Student A:**   I have a great impression of Beijing. I would like to go there again.

_____

Student B: Great! I've always wanted to go to Beijing. But would we be able to get airline tickets?

_____

Student A: We have to hurry. Otherwise, we won't be able to get them.

_____

G   Provide a brief history of your friendship with someone, including who your friend is, when and where you met, how long you have known each other, when you became friends, what your friend does well, what attributes your friend has, what he/she looks like, what you have in common, what you often do together, etc. **PRESENTATIONAL**

Dialogue 2: Turning Down an Invitation

Listening Comprehension

A   Listen to the Textbook Dialogue 2 audio, then mark these statements true or false. **INTERPRETIVE**

1 ____   Li You recognizes the caller's voice right away.

2 ____   Li You is not happy to get the call.

3 ____   Li You has never met the caller before.

4 ____   The caller wants to ask Li You to go out dancing with him.

5 ____   Li You tries to turn the caller down without directly saying so.

B   Listen to the Workbook Telephone Message. Based on what you hear, write a note in Chinese reconstructing the message. Make sure to include your friend's name, the caller's name, the purpose of the call, the time and place of the event, and the special request being made. **INTERPRETIVE & PRESENTATIONAL**

_____

_____

_____

_____

C ____   Listen to the Listening Rejoinder audio. After hearing the first speaker, select the best response from the four choices given by the second speaker. Indicate the number of your choice. **INTERPRETIVE**

Pinyin and Tone

A   Identify the characters with the same initials (either *j* or *x*) and write them in *pinyin*.

記　想　間　行　象

1   *j:*   _____

2   *x:*   _____

B Compare the tones of these characters. Indicate the tones with 1 (first tone), 2 (second tone), 3 (third tone), 4 (fourth tone), or 0 (neutral tone).

1 記 _____ 極 _____   3 房 _____ 放 _____

2 搬 _____ 班 _____   4 整 _____ 正 _____

Speaking

A Answer these questions in Chinese based on Textbook Dialogue 2. PRESENTATIONAL

1 According to the caller, when, where, and how did he meet Li You?

2 How did he get Li You's phone number?

3 What is the purpose of his phone call?

4 What is Li You planning to do over the next three weekends?

5 How does Li You end the conversation?

B In pairs, role-play inviting your partner to do something with you. Your partner should come up with different reasons to turn down the invitation. Both parties should be persistent but polite. INTERPERSONAL

Reading Comprehension

A If you combine the *wèn* in *wèntí* with the *hào* in *hàomǎ*, you have *wènhào*, as seen in exercise 1 below. Can you guess what the word *wènhào* means? Write the characters, *pinyin*, and English equivalent of each new word formed in this way. Consult a dictionary if necessary. INTERPRETIVE

1 "問題"的"問"＋"號碼"的"號"

→ 問＋號 → _____ _____ _____

2 "搬出去"的"搬"＋"我家"的"家"

→ 搬＋家 → _____ _____ _____

3 "吃藥"的"藥"＋"房間"的"房"

→ 藥＋房 → _____ _____ _____

4 "旅行"的"旅"＋"圖書館"的"館"

→ 旅＋館 → _____ _____ _____

5 "水電"的"電"＋"紅綠燈"的"燈"

→ 電＋燈 → _____ _____ _____

B Read this passage, then mark the statements true or false. **INTERPRETIVE**

李友：王朋，今天晚上想不想跟我去看
　　　電影？我請客。

王朋：看電影？

李友：對，很好看的電影，很多人想看，
　　　票我已經買好了。

王朋：你沒有車，票是怎麼買的？

李友：是剛才坐公共汽車去買的。我昨
　　　天考試考得不錯，我們好好兒玩
　　　兒玩兒吧。

王朋：可是我今天還沒打球呢。

李友：我知道你今天晚上想打球，明天
　　　再打吧。

王朋：好，沒問題，我和你去看電影。
幾點？

李友：八點⋯⋯還是八點一刻？讓我看
看電影票⋯⋯糟糕，電影票我忘
在公共汽車上了。

1 _____ Li You wants to go see a movie because she did well on her exam.

2 _____ Wang Peng accepts the invitation promptly.

3 _____ Wang Peng had previously planned to play ball this evening.

4 _____ We can assume that the movie theater will be half empty this evening.

5 _____ It is not clear from the tickets whether the movie starts at 8:00 p.m. or 8:15 p.m.

6 _____ Li You says that she found the movie tickets on the bus.

C | Read this passage, then mark the statements true or false. INTERPRETIVE

高文中：哎，李友，好久不見。明天有
一個音樂會，我買了兩張票。
一起去聽，好嗎？

李友：　你真客氣，可是，對不起，我
明天得先去買個冰箱，還得整
理房間。你還是跟白英愛去
吧。

高文中：你不是很喜歡聽音樂嗎？上個
月學校開音樂會，你早上七點
就去買票，費了很大力氣才買
到，對不對？

李友：　對，我很喜歡聽音樂，可是我
明天沒空兒。

高文中：哎，告訴你吧，李友，這兩張
票是我幫王朋買的。怎麼樣，
明天晚上不想整理房間了吧？

1 _____ 李友說明天晚上的音樂會沒有意思。

2 _____ 王朋找高文中幫他和李友買了兩張票，
可是沒有告訴李友。

3 _____ 高文中今天早上七點就去買票了。

4 _____ 李友說她剛買了一個冰箱，可是冰箱現
在不在她的房間裡。

5 _____ 李友上個月去聽學校的音樂會了。

6 _____ 上個月學校開音樂會，很多人不想去。

7 _____ 高文中覺得李友明天晚上不會在家整
理房間，她會跟王朋去聽音樂會。

D What does the store sell? List three items.

_____

_____

_____

A In addition to 打掃, provide three more words or phrases that start with the character 打, along with the meaning of each of them in English.

1 _____ _____

2 _____ _____

3 _____ _____

4 _____ _____

B Form a character by fitting the given components together as indicated, then provide a word or phrase in which that character appears. Follow the example below.

上邊一個"田"，下邊一個"力"是"男朋友"的"男"。

1 左邊一個"亻"，右邊一個"兩"是 _____
  的 _____ 。

2 左邊一個"言"，右邊一個"己"是 _____
  的 _____ 。

3 左邊一個"木"，右邊一個"幾"是_____
  的 _____ 。

4 左邊一個"石"，右邊一個"馬"是 _____
  的 _____ 。

5 上邊一個"日"，下邊一個"生"是 _____
  的 _____ 。

C Answer these questions according to your own circumstances. **INTERPERSONAL**

1 Q: 你記得不記得你上個星期五吃了些什麼東西？

A: _____

2 Q: 你想得起來想不起來你中學英文老師叫什麼名字？

A: _____

3 Q: 你知道不知道你爸爸、媽媽的手機號碼？

A: _____

D Your friend, an animal obedience trainer, has a client in Chinatown who needs help training his dog. The dog only follows simple commands in Chinese, and your friend asks you to teach him some common commands. Write down the proper commands in Chinese based on each image. **PRESENTATIONAL**

1

_____

2

_____

3

_____

4

_____

5

_____

6

_____

7

_____

8

_____

E | Translate these sentences into Chinese. **PRESENTATIONAL**

1 Student A: When did you move out of the dorm?

_____

Student B: I moved out in February.

_____

2 Student A: Who's the woman sitting next to Little Wang? I can't remember.

_____

Student B: I don't know her. I've never met her before.

_____

3 Student A: I'm going to be traveling for a month. Please remember to clean the house once a week.

_____

Student B: No problem. I won't forget. Have fun. Call my cell phone if you need anything.

_____

F | List three lines that you could use if you needed to end a phone conversation without hurting the other person's feelings. **PRESENTATIONAL**

1 _____

2 _____

3 _____

G | List three ways to decline a date indirectly and politely. **PRESENTATIONAL**

1 _____

2 _____

3 _____

H Describe your perfect date, including the time, the location, and the activity. PRESENTATIONAL

_____

_____

I Write a story in Chinese based on the four images below. Make sure that your story has a beginning, middle, and end, and that the transition from one image to the next is smooth and logical. PRESENTATIONAL

1

3

_____

_____

_____

_____

_____

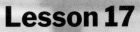

租房子
Renting an Apartment

 Check off the following items as you learn them.

Useful Expressions

[ ] My dorm is very noisy.

[ ] It's really inconvenient!

[ ] The apartment is already furnished.

[ ] Do I have to pay a deposit?

[ ] No pets are allowed in our apartments.

Cultural Norms

[ ] Campus dorms

[ ] Renting an apartment

[ ] Popular pets

As you progress through the lesson, note other useful expressions and cultural norms you would like to learn.

_____

_____

_____

Narrative: Finding a Better Place

Audio

Listening Comprehension

A Listen to the Textbook Narrative audio, then circle the most appropriate choice. INTERPRETIVE

1 How long has Wang Peng been living in his dorm?

   a two weeks   c two semesters

   b two years   d two months

2 Wang Peng's dorm has many problems, but he isn't bothered by

   a the price.   c the noise.

   b the size.   d the location.

3 How long has Wang Peng been looking for an apartment?

   a about a week   c about a year

   b about a month   d about a semester

4 How many rooms does the advertised apartment have?

   a three   c four

   b five   d two

B Listen to the Workbook Narrative audio of a voice mail Wang Peng just received, then mark these statements true or false. INTERPRETIVE

1 _____ The speaker is probably a friend of Wang Peng's.

2 _____ The speaker thinks that he and Wang Peng would be good roommates.

3 _____ The speaker would like to move off campus.

4 _____ The speaker is trying to persuade Wang Peng to move into a different dorm.

5 _____ The speaker thinks it's great to be able to cook for oneself.

C Reply to the caller in the Workbook Narrative audio on Wang Peng's behalf. INTERPERSONAL

_____

_____

_____

D _____ Listen to the Listening Rejoinder audio. After hearing the first speaker, select the best response from the four choices given by the second speaker. Indicate the number of your choice. INTERPRETIVE

Pinyin and Tone

A Identify the characters with the same initials (either *z* or *zh*) and write them in *pinyin*.

準　紙　租　走　住

1　*z:* _____

2　*zh:* _____

B Compare the tones of these characters. Indicate the tones with 1 (first tone), 2 (second tone), 3 (third tone), 4 (fourth tone), or 0 (neutral tone).

1　連 _____ 臉 _____

2　寓 _____ 魚 _____

3　報 _____ 保 _____

4　附 _____ 服 _____

Speaking

A Answer these questions in Chinese based on the Textbook Narrative. **PRESENTATIONAL**

1　Why does Wang Peng want to move out of his dorm?

2　How long has Wang Peng been looking for an apartment?

3　How far from school is the advertised apartment?

4　What other information does the ad include apart from the apartment's location?

B In pairs, discuss where you live, how far it is from school, and why you do or don't like your current place. **INTERPERSONAL**

C This is Little Xia's place. In pairs, talk about the rooms in the apartment and the furniture in the main rooms. **INTERPERSONAL**

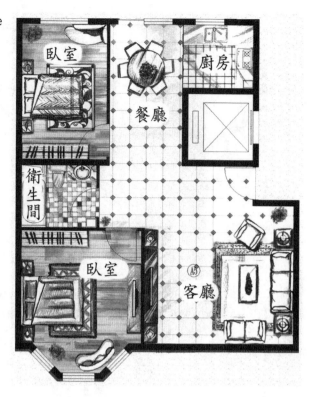

臥室 　 廚房

餐廳

衛生間

臥室

客廳

Reading Comprehension

A If you combine the *wǎn* in *wǎnshang* with the *bào* in *bàozhǐ*, you have *wǎnbào*, as seen in Exercise 1 below. Can you guess what the word *wǎnbào* means? Write the characters, *pinyin*, and English equivalent of each new word formed in this way. Consult a dictionary if necessary.

1 "晚上"的"晚"＋"報紙"的"報"

→ 晚＋報 → _____ _____ _____

2 "寫信"的"信"＋"一張紙"的"紙"

→ 信＋紙 → _____ _____ _____

3 "一套"的"套"＋"房間"的"間"

→ 套＋間 → _____ _____ _____

4 "衛生間"的"衛生"＋"一張紙"的"紙"

→ 衛生＋紙 → _____ _____

5 "廚房"的"廚"＋"師傅"的"師"

→ 廚＋師 → _____ _____ _____

B Read this passage, then mark the statements true or false. **INTERPRETIVE**

　　小馬在學生宿舍住了兩個學期了。因為他的房間很小，放不下兩張床，所以他一個人住。宿舍裡有餐廳、圖書室、電腦室，還有洗衣房，非常方便。小馬不太會做飯，又很喜歡認識新朋友，所以覺得住宿舍對他很合適。他聽說在校外租房子比住宿舍便宜，但是得跟別人一起住，還得自己做飯，不太方便。所以他現在還不知道下個學期要不要搬出去住。

1 _____ 小馬是兩個學期以前搬進學生宿舍的。

2 _____ 雖然房間裡有兩張床，可是沒有別人住在小馬的房間裡。

3 _____ 小馬想用電腦的時候，得去學校的電腦中心。

4 _____ 小馬覺得自己做飯沒有在餐廳吃飯方便。

5 _____ 住學校宿舍雖然比住在學校外邊貴，可是很方便。

6 _____ 小馬還不清楚他下個學期要住在哪兒。

C Read this passage, then mark the statements true or false. INTERPRETIVE

　　我是今年寒假搬進我現在住的公寓的。公寓離學校很近，開車只要五分鐘，買東西也很方便。雖然臥室不太大，可是廚房和客廳都很漂亮，而且傢俱都是新的，每個月只要五百塊錢。公寓這麼好，怎麼這麼便宜呢？我想這個問題想了三個月了，上個星期才聽說很多住過這個公寓的人都會生病，而且如果住的時間長，病就會越來越重，但是一搬出這個公寓，病就好了。所以這兒的房租一定得便宜，要不然沒有人住。我應該怎麼辦呢？雖然現在我的身體很健康，可是我得好好兒想想，要不要準備搬家？

1 _____ The narrator's apartment is inexpensive and conveniently located.

2 _____ All of the rooms in the apartment are spacious and beautifully furnished.

3 _____ Similar apartments elsewhere in the city are considerably more expensive.

4 _____ Before the narrator moved into the apartment, he talked to many former tenants of this apartment building.

D Read the passage in (C), then answer the questions by circling the most appropriate choice.
INTERPRETIVE

1 What happened to many of the people who once lived in the apartment building?
   a They couldn't find doctors when they got sick.
   b They couldn't move out when they got sick.
   c Their health was temporarily affected.
   d Their health was permanently affected.

2 **The narrator found out the truth behind the low rent**

    a over winter break.

    b last week.

    c three months ago.

    d in March.

3 **At the end of the passage, the narrator sounds**

    a bitter.

    b ill.

    c indifferent.

    d conflicted.

E Look at the floor plan and answer the following questions.

1 請用英文寫出這個公寓有什麼房間：

_____

2 "主臥室"的英文是：

_____

A Write the radical 宀 in the character 寓 and three more characters with the same radical. Then compound each character with another one to form a word or a phrase, and provide their meanings in English (write the radical in 1).

1

3 _____ _____

2 _____ _____

4 _____ _____

B What rooms does your apartment, house, or dorm have? List up to eight of them in Chinese.
PRESENTATIONAL

1 _____

5 _____

2 _____

6 _____

3 _____

7 _____

4 _____

8 _____

C Answer these questions in Chinese according to your own circumstances. **INTERPERSONAL**

1 Q: 你住的地方是學校宿舍、房子、還是公寓？
吵不吵？

A: _____

2 Q: 你自己一個人住還是跟別人一起住？

A: _____

3 Q: 你住的地方帶不帶傢俱？

A: _____

4 Q: 有沒有自己的衛生間？

A: _____

5 Q: 有沒有廚房？可以做飯嗎？

A: _____

6 Q: 上學、坐車、買東西方便不方便？

A: _____

7 Q: 附近有什麼飯館、商店？

A: _____

8 Q: 臥室大不大？能放下一個大電視嗎？

A: _____

9 Q: 你在現在住的地方住了多長時間了？

A: _____

10 Q: 下個學期你準備搬家嗎？為什麼？

A: _____

D Answer these questions about your commute in Chinese. INTERPERSONAL

1 Q: 你今天是怎麼去學校的？走路、開車、
還是坐車？

A: _____

2 Q: 你今天是什麼時候到學校的？

A: _____

3 Q: 你今天是自己一個人還是跟同學一起去
學校的？

A: _____

4 Q: 你住的地方離學校遠不遠？走路走多長時間？/開車開多長時間？/坐公共汽車坐多長時間？

A: _____

E The IC cast members have been learning new skills in their free time. Form questions-and-answers about their new endeavors based on the information given, following the example below.

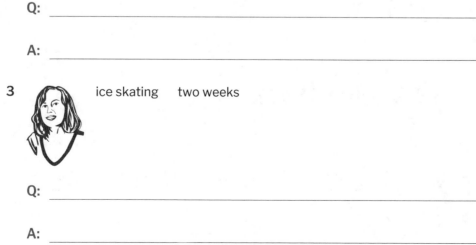

cooking   three months

Q: 王朋學做飯學了多長時間了？

A: 王朋學做飯學了三個月了。

1   driving   one month

Q: _____

A: _____

2   English   half a year

Q: _____

A: _____

3   ice skating   two weeks

Q: _____

A: _____

4 computer   five days

Q: _____

A: _____

F Based on the images, use 得下 to describe how much you can eat or drink, following the example below. **PRESENTATIONAL**

 Q: 你吃得下幾個餃子？
A: 我吃得下六個餃子。

1

Q: _____

A: _____

2

Q: _____

A: _____

3

Q: _____

A: _____

Translate these sentences into Chinese. **PRESENTATIONAL**

1 **Student A:** My apartment is very big. There's enough room for four people.

_____

Student B: My room is small. It can't even fit a large bed.

_____

2 **Student A:** The place where I live is close to the stores. It's convenient for going shopping.

_____

Student B: Really? How long does it take to walk to the stores?

_____

Student A: It only takes three minutes to walk there.

_____

3 **Student A:** You've been living here for a little over a month. How's it going?

_____

Student B: I would like to move out.

_____

Student A: What's the matter?

_____

Student B: It's too noisy. I can't get a good night's sleep.

_____

Dialogue: Calling about an Apartment for Rent

Listening Comprehension

A   Listen to the Textbook Dialogue audio, then mark these statements true or false. **INTERPRETIVE**

1 ____   There isn't any furniture in the living room.

2 ____   Wang Peng thinks the apartment is a little expensive.

3 ____   There don't seem to be any chairs in the bedroom.

4 ____   Wang Peng will most likely study in the living room.

5 ____   Wang Peng won't have to pay for utilities.

6 ____   Wang Peng's first payment will be $1,600.

B   Listen to the Workbook Narrative audio, then circle the most appropriate choice. **INTERPRETIVE**

1   **Little Huang's apartment is not very**

    a   expensive.

    b   convenient.

    c   noisy.

    d   large.

2   **Little Huang probably has a**

    a   three-room apartment.

    b   studio apartment.

    c   four-room apartment.

    d   two-room apartment.

3   **Little Huang doesn't have a**

    a   bed.

    b   desk.

    c   chair.

    d   bookcase.

4   **Little Huang wishes his apartment were less**

    a   expensive.

    b   noisy.

    c   cramped.

    d   far from work.

C Listen to the Workbook Dialogue audio, then mark these statements true or false. **INTERPRETIVE**

1 _____ The bedroom is the nicest room in the apartment.

2 _____ The man likes the bedroom and intends to spend most of his time there.

3 _____ The room the man intends to sleep in is well furnished.

4 _____ We can assume that nobody will be using the desk.

5 _____ Pets are allowed in this apartment building.

6 _____ Meimei likes to eat takeout food.

7 _____ Meimei is the man's faithful, devoted servant.

D _____ Listen to the Listening Rejoinder audio. After hearing the first speaker, select the best response from the four choices given by the second speaker. Indicate the number of your choice. **INTERPRETIVE**

Pinyin and Tone

A Identify the characters with the same finals (either *ü* or *u*) and write them in *pinyin*.

出 租 寓 俱 住

1 *ü:* _____

2 *u:* _____

B Compare the tones of these characters. Indicate the tones with 1 (first tone), 2 (second tone), 3 (third tone), 4 (fourth tone), or 0 (neutral tone).

1 靜 _____ 淨 _____

2 幣 _____ 鼻 _____

3 樣 _____ 癢 _____

4 元 _____ 遠 _____

A Answer these questions in Chinese based on the Textbook Dialogue. PRESENTATIONAL

1 What furniture comes with the apartment?

2 How much is the rent per month?

3 What kind of discount did the landlady offer Wang Peng?

4 How much is the deposit?

5 Do you think that Wang Peng has ever had pets? Why or why not?

B In pairs, role-play a tenant asking a landlord about an apartment for rent. Make sure you get all the details about the apartment, such as how far the apartment is from school; how many rooms it has; whether it comes furnished; how much the rent, utilities, and deposit will be; and whether pets are allowed. Set up an appointment to see the apartment in person. INTERPERSONAL

C Describe your residence based on a photo or drawing. Mention how many rooms it has, where it is located and what is nearby, how far it is from school, what furniture it has, etc. PRESENTATIONAL

Reading Comprehension

A If you combine the *lěng* in *hěn lěng* with the *jìng* in *ānjìng*, you have *lěngjìng*, as seen in exercise 1 below. Can you guess what the word *lěngjìng* means? Write the characters, *pinyin*, and English equivalent of each new word formed in this way. Consult a dictionary if necessary. INTERPRETIVE

1 "很冷"的"冷" + "安靜"的"靜"

→ 冷 + 靜 → _____ _____ _____

2 "安靜"的"靜" + "水電"的"電"

→ 靜 + 電 → _____ _____ _____

3 "報紙"的"紙" + "人民幣"的"幣"

→ 紙＋幣 → _____ _____ _____

4 "學習"的"學" + "水電費"的"費"

→ 學＋費 → _____ _____ _____

5 "出租"的"租" + "押金"的"金"

→ 租＋金 → _____ _____ _____

B Read this passage, then mark the statements true or false. INTERPRETIVE

小張在學校宿舍住了兩年了，最近才搬出
來，在學校附近租了一套公寓，公寓裡什麼傢
俱都沒有。朋友們告訴他什麼都不用買，因為
他們有很多傢俱。他們送給了小張一張書桌，
兩個書架和一張床。那張床特別漂亮，哪個傢
俱店都買不到。他們還說，要是小張還要別的
東西，什麼時候給他們打電話都可以。

1 ____ Little Zhang has lived in his apartment for two years.

2 ____ The apartment is not furnished.

3 ____ Little Zhang's friends want to know what furniture he wants to buy.

4 ____ Little Zhang is wondering what furniture store he should visit to find a beautiful bed.

5 ____ Little Zhang will not have to spend any money on furniture.

6 ____ Little Zhang's friends want to know when he will call them.

小黃上個月在學校附近找了一套小公寓，一房一廳，還帶傢俱。房租每個月只要五百二十塊。小黃覺得比住在學校宿舍便宜多了，所以就搬進去了。可是他搬進去以後才知道，他每個月得付九十塊錢的水電費。小黃覺得太貴了。昨天他又找到了一套房子，雖然離學校有一點兒遠，可是很安靜，房租每個月五百四十塊，不用付水電費。小黃對那套公寓很有興趣，想下個星期搬進去。可是因為他在現在的公寓只住了一個月，如果現在搬出去,付的押金就拿不回來了。

1 ____ Little Huang has lived in his current apartment for one semester.

2 ____ Little Huang thought his current apartment was inexpensive when he moved in.

3 ____ The on-campus dorms cost $520 per month.

4 ____ Little Huang has to pay at least $610 a month for his current apartment.

5 ____ Little Huang's current apartment is far from campus.

6 ____ Once he moves into the new apartment, he will pay only $540 per month.

7 ____ Little Huang's new apartment is quiet but relatively far from campus.

8 ____ When he moves out of his current apartment, he will get his deposit back.

D Read this passage, then create an image by hand or with a computer on a separate piece of paper, based on the given information. INTERPRETIVE

　　李先生家樓下有一個客廳，一個廁所，一個廚房。客廳裡的傢俱不多，就一個沙發，一張咖啡桌。你看，李先生正坐在沙發上看報紙呢！廚房裡有一張飯桌和四把椅子。樓上有兩個臥室，一個衛生間。每個臥室都有一張床，李太太正在打掃整理右邊的臥室。左邊的臥室是誰的呢？我想起來了，是他們兒子的房間。他怎麼躺在床上呢？糟糕，他對房子附近的花過敏，眼睛很不舒服！……你看，他們家的狗小白正在房子外邊玩呢。小白眼睛大大的，嘴也大大的，非常可愛。

E Between these two rentals, which would you pick? Give your reasons in Chinese. INTERPERSONAL

房屋租售

房屋出租

三房兩廳
兩個廁所
有冰箱，洗衣機
月租：$1375
有意請電：425-754-
XXXX

房屋出租
$180-$350

電視CABLE，近公車站
有意者請電：206-
682-XXXX

A You have just learned the word 興趣. Write the radical 走 in the character 趣 and two characters with the same radical. Then compound each character with another one to form a word or phrase, and provide their meanings in English (write the radical in 1).

1

2 _____ _____

3 _____ _____

B Form a character by fitting the given components together as indicated, then provide a word or phrase in which that character appears. Follow the example below.

左邊一個"亻"，右邊一個"更"是"方便"的"便"。

1 左邊一個"口"，右邊一個"少"是 _____
   的 _____ 。

2 左邊一個"禾"，右邊一個"且"是 _____
   的 _____ 。

3 左邊一個"亻"，右邊一個"寸"是 _____
   的 _____ 。

4 左邊一個"氵"，右邊一個"少"是 _____
   的 _____ 。

5 上邊一個"加"，下邊一個"木"是 _____
   的 _____ 。

C List four pieces of furniture in your current residence.

1 _____   3 _____

2 _____   4 _____

D Use an online currency converter to answer the following questions. Cite the website you used and provide the date of your search. **INTERPERSONAL**

1 Q: 一百元美元能換多少人民幣？

   A: _____

2 Q: 一百元人民幣能換多少美元？

   A: _____

3 網站：_____

4 日期：_____

E Rewrite these sentences using "都/也," following the example below. **PRESENTATIONAL**

小夏不認識小王、小白、小張、小高……。

→ 小夏誰都/也不認識。

1 老師上午、中午、下午、晚上都沒空。

_____

2 這個房間沒有桌子、椅子、床……。

_____

3 我弟弟喝茶、喝水、喝可樂、喝咖啡，也喝
果汁。

_____

4 李老師對小王的印象不好，對小張、小白、
小高的印象也不好。

_____

F 如果你想租房子，租房子以前，你會問房東哪
些問題？ **PRESENTATIONAL**

1 _____

2 _____

3 _____

4 _____

5 _____

6 _____

7 _____

8 _____

G 你的朋友正想租房子，下邊是報紙上的一個出租廣告，你覺得對你的朋友很合適。可是你的朋友看不懂英文，請你用中文告訴他廣告上說了些什麼。 **PRESENTATIONAL**

Apt for Rent
3 BR, 1 LR, 2 BA, furnished

quiet
walk to Univ
close to bus stop, shopping, and park

$965 a month, utilities included
no pets allowed

555-5555

_____

_____

_____

_____

H Translate these sentences and the passage into Chinese. **PRESENTATIONAL**

1 Q: This living room is so clean.

_____

A: It's too clean! It has nothing, not even a piece of furniture or a piece of paper.

_____

2 Q: What are you interested in?

_____

A: I am interested in keeping pets.

_____

3 I've been living with my friend for more than two years. Our apartment is furnished and very close to school, the park, and the bus stop. The rent is less expensive than in the dorms. I like where I live. My friend is also very nice to me. He cleans the house once a week and often hosts dance parties. Even my mother likes the place where I live. But I may have to move out next semester. It's not because it's so noisy that I cannot sleep well, and it's not because I am allergic to my friend's dog. It's because my friend's cousin is moving in and the place is too small for three people. It's difficult to find a suitable and affordable apartment. I could ask my friend if he'd like to find a house that's a little bigger.

_____

_____

_____

_____

_____

I List three things that you like and dislike, respectively, about your current residence.
PRESENTATIONAL

喜歡

1 _____

2 _____

3 _____

不喜歡

1 _____

2 _____

3 _____

J Based on the lists in the previous exercise, describe your ideal living quarters. PRESENTATIONAL

_____

_____

_____

_____

K Write a story based on the four images below. Make sure that your story has a beginning, middle, and end, and that the transition from one image to the next is smooth and logical. PRESENTATIONAL

1

2

3

4

_____

_____

_____

_____

_____

運動
Sports

 Check off the following items as you learn them.

Useful Expressions

[ ] I exercise three times a week.

[ ] That's way too much hassle.

[ ] That's really dangerous.

[ ] There's nothing I can do.

[ ] Hurry, turn the TV on.

Cultural Norms

[ ] Popular sports

[ ] Morning exercises

[ ] Diet and weight

As you progress through the lesson, note other useful expressions and cultural norms you would like to learn.

_____

_____

_____

Dialogue 1: Getting in Shape

Listening Comprehension

A Listen to the Textbook Dialogue 1 audio, then mark these statements true or false. **INTERPRETIVE**

1 ____ Wang Peng says he has been putting on weight.

2 ____ Gao Wenzhong wants to start exercising right away.

3 ____ Gao Wenzhong hasn't exercised in two years.

4 ____ Wang Peng suggests that Gao Wenzhong take up martial arts.

5 ____ Gao Wenzhong thinks playing basketball is too expensive.

B Listen to the Workbook Telephone Message Bai Ying'ai left for Gao Wenzhong, then circle the most appropriate choice. **INTERPRETIVE**

1 Bai Ying'ai calls Gao Wenzhong to ask him to
   a come to her birthday party.
   b play tennis with her.
   c have breakfast with her.
   d meet her classmate.

2 Bai Ying'ai suggests that Gao Wenzhong
   a buy a tennis racket.
   b buy some tennis balls.
   c hire a tennis coach.
   d get a pair of tennis shoes.

3 Who else might come?
   a Bai Ying'ai's father
   b Bai Ying'ai's classmate
   c Bai Ying'ai's friend Wang Peng
   d Bai Ying'ai's teacher

4 Bai Ying'ai thinks that Gao Wenzhong may not want to go because
   a tennis shoes are expensive.
   b he doesn't eat breakfast.
   c he can't get up early.
   d he isn't a sports enthusiast.

Listen to the Listening Rejoinder audio. After hearing the first speaker, select the best response from the four choices given by the second speaker. Indicate the number of your choice. **INTERPRETIVE**

Pinyin and Tone

A Identify the characters with the same finals (either *an* or *ang*) and write them in *pinyin*.

當　然　單　籃　胖

1 *an:* _____

2 *ang:* _____

B Compare the tones of these characters. Indicate the tones with 1 (first tone), 2 (second tone), 3 (third tone), 4 (fourth tone), or 0 (neutral tone).

1 胖 _____ 旁 _____   3 單 _____ 蛋 _____

2 簡 _____ 間 _____   4 籃 _____ 懶 _____

Speaking

A Answer these questions in Chinese based on Textbook Dialogue 1. **PRESENTATIONAL**

1 According to Wang Peng, why has Gao Wenzhong gained weight?

2 How often and for how long does Wang Peng recommend that Gao Wenzhong exercise?

3 How long has it been since Gao Wenzhong exercised?

4 What sports does Wang Peng recommend?

5 What excuse does Gao Wenzhong give for disliking jogging?

6 Why does Wang Peng recommend swimming?

7 What is Wang Peng's conclusion?

B In pairs, have a conversation about exercise routines. Ask your partner if he/she exercises, how often, what kind of exercise he/she does, and why he/she likes that kind of exercise. **INTERPERSONAL**

A If you combine the *pǎo* in *pǎo bù* with the *chē* in *qìchē*, you have *pǎochē*, as seen in Exercise 1 below. Can you guess what the word *pǎochē* means? Write the characters, *pinyin*, and English equivalent of each new word formed in this way. Consult a dictionary if necessary. INTERPRETIVE

1 "跑步"的"跑"+"汽車"的"車"

→ 跑+車 → _____ _____ _____

2 "上網"的"網"+"人民"的"民"

→ 網+民 → _____ _____ _____

3 "一把花"的"花"+"籃球"的"籃"

→ 花+籃 → _____ _____ _____

4 "游泳"的"泳"+"衣服"的"衣"

→ 泳+衣 → _____ _____ _____

5 "危險"的"危"+"樓下"的"樓"

→ 危+樓 → _____ _____ _____

B Read this passage, then mark the statements true or false. INTERPRETIVE

　　大明是小明的哥哥，他們都喜歡運動。大明每個星期打一次籃球，有時候還跟朋友一起去打網球。要是朋友都很忙，不能去打球，大明就自己一個人去跑步。小明跟大明不一樣，已經兩年沒有運動了，只喜歡看別人運動。他覺得球賽比什麼都好看，電視裡一有籃球比賽或者網球賽，小明就坐在沙發上看，有時候連飯都不想吃。大明今年三十五歲，但因為常常運動，身體好極了。小明今年只有二十五歲，可是越來越胖。大明小明兩個人在一起，不認識他們的人常說大明是弟弟，小明是哥哥。小明不懂為什麼他和哥哥都喜歡運動，可是身體沒有哥哥那麼好。

1 ____ The older brother looks younger than the younger brother.

2 ____ Running is Big Ming's favorite kind of exercise.

3 ____ The last time Little Ming exercised was two years ago.

4 ____ When there is a ball game on TV, Little Ming doesn't want to watch anything else.

5 ____ Little Ming has gained weight because he doesn't eat regularly.

6 ____ Both brothers love sports, but in very different ways.

C | Read this dialogue, then answer the questions. **INTERPRETIVE**

哥哥：你最近常常生病，身體越來越糟糕，要想身體好，就得運動。運動不用多，做一種就夠了。

弟弟：一種就夠了？我做過好幾種運動，可是一點兒用都沒有。半年前我就開始打網球了。

哥哥：網球是一種很好的運動。你現在跟誰一起打？

弟弟：我五個月沒打網球了。我覺得游泳更有意思，所以打了兩次網球，就去游泳了。

哥哥：游泳也不錯。你現在在哪兒游泳？

弟弟：我四個月沒游泳了。我游了兩個多星期的泳，覺得還是打籃球方便，就開始打籃球了。

哥哥：你不說我也知道，你打了幾次籃球，覺得沒意思，就好幾個月沒打了，對不對？我現在才知道，你的身體為什麼這麼不好。

1 What is the older brother's initial advice to the younger brother on losing weight?

_____

2 What sports has the younger brother tried recently?

_____

3 For how long did the younger brother play tennis?

_____

4 When did the younger brother stop going swimming?

_____

5 Why do you think none of these sports has worked for the younger brother?

_____

6 Does the older brother think that his younger brother is likely to change his habits and get healthier?

_____

D According to the TV guide provided, when can you watch basketball? **INTERPRETIVE**

_____

BTV 6
11:15 體壇風雲
13:15 奧運故事365
16:00 籃球精彩回放
21:25 直播：天天體育

A Compound the second character in these words with another character to form a new word or phrase, and provide their meanings in English.

1 當然 _____ _____

2 淹死 _____ _____

3 願意 _____ _____

4 籃球 _____ _____

B Answer these questions and explain your opinions. **INTERPERSONAL**

1 Q: 什麼運動很危險？

   A: _____

2 Q: 什麼運動很簡單？

   A: _____

3 Q: 什麼運動很麻煩？

   A: _____

4 Q: 什麼運動得花很多時間？

   A: _____

5 Q: 什麼運動得花很多錢？

   A: _____

C Little Wang has been so busy studying this semester that he's neglected doing anything else. Based on the information provided, describe what he hasn't had time to do, and for how long, following the example below. PRESENTATIONAL

 ❌ two months

小王兩個月沒運動了。

1  ❌ a week

_____

2  ❌ three months

_____

3  ❌ thirty-six hours

_____

4  ❌ one semester

_____

Answer these questions according to your own circumstances. **INTERPERSONAL**

1 Q: 你覺得哪一個漢字好寫？哪一個漢字難寫？

   A: _____

2 Q: 你覺得哪一個生詞好懂？哪一個生詞難懂？

   A: _____

3 Q: 你覺得哪一個字的音好發？哪一個字的音難發？

   A: _____

E Fill in the blanks with the appropriate phrases. **INTERPRETIVE**

學下去　住下去　跑下去　寫下去　忙下去

1 這個公寓對我很合適，明年我想 _____
_____ ，不想搬出去。

2 他給一個外國朋友寫電郵寫了很多年了，
還會 _____ 。

3 中文非常有意思，我下個學期一定 _____
_____ 。

4 你最近忙得不能好好兒吃飯、睡覺，再
這麼 _____ ，一定會生病，
多休息幾天吧。

F Translate these sentences and the passage into Chinese. PRESENTATIONAL

1 Q: Why don't you like swimming? Are you afraid of water?

  _____

  A: Of course not. I feel that going swimming is a lot of trouble.

  _____

2 Q: You studied dancing for three years. Why didn't you continue?

  _____

  A: I was too tired, and I didn't want to continue.

  _____

  Q: How long has it been since you danced?

  _____

  A: It's been more than six months.

  _____

3 I have studied Chinese for more than seven months. My teacher asked us to listen to the audio for half an hour every day. But I haven't for more than a week. There's a test tomorrow. I'd better review thoroughly and hope I ace the test.

  _____

  _____

  _____

Dialogue 2: Watching American Football

Listening Comprehension

A Listen to the Textbook Dialogue 2 audio, then mark these statements true or false. **INTERPRETIVE**

1 ____ Wang Hong has watched soccer in the past.

2 ____ Wang Hong is unfamiliar with American football.

3 ____ Gao Xiaoyin's boyfriend loves watching American football.

4 ____ Wang Hong becomes instantly hooked on American football.

B Listen to the Workbook Dialogue audio, then mark these statements true or false. **INTERPRETIVE**

1 ____ The woman doesn't believe that Gao Wenzhong went to play tennis.

2 ____ Gao Wenzhong may not like playing tennis much, but he likes his tennis partner.

3 ____ The man gives high marks to Gao Wenzhong for his positive attitude.

4 ____ Gao Wenzhong gave up tennis after one lesson.

5 ____ The woman thinks that Gao Wenzhong will succeed in losing weight.

C ____ Listen to the Listening Rejoinder audio. After hearing the first speaker, select the best response from the four choices given by the second speaker. Indicate the number of your choice. **INTERPRETIVE**

Pinyin and Tone

A Identify the characters with the same initials (either *sh* or *q*) and write them in *pinyin*.

球 手 受 秋 收

1 *sh:* _____

2 *q:* _____

Compare the tones of these characters. Indicate the tones with 1 (first tone), 2 (second tone), 3 (third tone), 4 (fourth tone), or 0 (neutral tone).

1 抱 _____ 報 _____   3 足 _____ 租 _____

2 擔 _____ 單 _____   4 踢 _____ 體 _____

Speaking

A Answer these questions in Chinese based on Textbook Dialogue 2. PRESENTATIONAL

1 How much time does Wang Hong spend watching TV and why?

2 What does Gao Xiaoyin want to watch?

3 What two differences between American football and soccer does Gao Xiaoyin mention?

4 Why does Wang Hong want to switch channels?

5 Do you think Gao Xiaoyin's boyfriend likes to watch American football? Why or why not?

B In pairs, have a conversation about TV-watching habits. Ask your partner how often he/she watches TV and whether he/she watches sports on TV. If so, which sports does he/she watch? INTERPERSONAL

C In pairs, discuss whether you like or dislike watching American football, and explain your reasons. PRESENTATIONAL

Reading Comprehension

A If you combine the *sài* in *bǐsài* with the *pǎo* in *pǎo bù*, you have *sàipǎo*, as seen in exercise 1 below. Can you guess what the word *sàipǎo* means? Write the characters, *pinyin*, and English equivalent of each new word formed in this way. Consult a dictionary if necessary. INTERPRETIVE

1 "比賽"的"賽"+"跑步"的"跑"

→ 賽+跑 → _____ _____ _____

2 "比賽"的"賽"+"唱歌"的"歌"

→ 賽+歌 → _____ _____ _____

3 "水平"的"平"+"手"

→ 平+手 → _____ _____ _____

4 "天氣"的"氣"+"壓壞"的"壓"

→ 氣+壓 → _____ _____ _____

5 "運動"的"動"+"寵物"的"物"

→ 動+物 → _____ _____ _____

B | Read this passage, then mark the statements true or false. INTERPRETIVE

　　為了提高自己的中文水平，白先生每天下午開車到圖書館去看兩個多小時的中國電影。今天吃完午飯他想去圖書館，才想起來自己的汽車讓表弟開回家去了。他打電話請表弟把車開回來，可是表弟的太太說，車讓他開到機場去了。白先生知道今天不能去圖書館了。

1 ___ Mr. Bai is a native Chinese speaker.

2 ___ Mr. Bai spends at least two hours in the library every day.

3 ___ Mr. Bai's home is not within walking distance of the library.

4 ___ Mr. Bai drove his cousin's car to the library yesterday.

5 ___ When Mr. Bai called, his cousin wasn't home.

6 ___ Mr. Bai still plans to go to the library later this afternoon.

Read the passage, then answer the questions in English. **INTERPRETIVE**

張英和妹妹都喜歡打網球。張英每個星期六下午打兩個小時的球，然後回家吃晚飯。上個星期六她沒打，因為球拍叫妹妹拿去了。妹妹那天要跟朋友打球，她覺得姐姐的球拍比她的好。今天又是星期六。張英告訴媽媽她晚上七點半才會回家吃晚飯，因為上個星期六她沒打球，所以今天要打四個小時的球。

1 Why didn't Zhang Ying play tennis last Saturday?

_____

2 What did Zhang Ying's sister do last Saturday?

_____

3 When do you think Zhang Ying will start playing tennis today?

_____

4 Does Zhang Ying usually have dinner at 7:30 on Saturdays?

_____

5 For how much longer than usual will Zhang Ying play tennis today?

_____

D Read the passage, then mark the statements true or false. **INTERPRETIVE**

高小音的男朋友很喜歡運動。他每天游一個小時的泳，每個星期打一次籃球。他沒有踢過美式足球，可是美式足球是他最喜歡看的球賽。高小音剛從英國來美國的時候，不太懂美式足球。可是現在跟男朋友一樣，都愛看美式足球，電視上一有美式足球賽，他們倆就連飯也忘了吃。

1 _____ Gao Xiaoyin's boyfriend is great at swimming, basketball, and American football.

2 _____ Gao Xiaoyin's boyfriend exercises at least seven hours every week.

3 _____ Gao Xiaoyin was an American football fan before she came to the United States.

4 _____ For Gao Xiaoyin, her boyfriend's enthusiasm for American football was contagious.

5 _____ Before watching American football games on TV, Gao Xiaoyin and her boyfriend usually have a meal out.

E Here's today's TV guide for the sports channels. Circle any soccer programs you see listed.
INTERPRETIVE

體育電視菜單

0100 MLB美國職棒大聯盟： 費城人對亞特蘭大勇士	2030 2017印第安維爾斯網球賽： 費德勒對納達爾
1000 （直播）MLB美國職棒大聯盟： 舊金山巨人對亞利桑那響尾蛇	2130 MLB美國職棒大聯盟： 舊金山巨人對亞利桑那響尾蛇
1300 足球：進球大匯串	0030 （首播）WWE HEAT
1330 英超指南	0130 第八屆冬季X GAMES - 趣味 鏡頭
1400 （首播）2017年世界排球大獎賽： 阿根廷對澳大利亞 （第二場）	0155 （直播）2017/18年西班牙甲級 足球聯賽： 皇家馬德里對巴塞罗那
1530 MLB美國職棒大聯盟： 舊金山巨人對亞利桑那響尾蛇	0400 亞洲賽車集錦
1830 （首播） ESPN趣味野外競賽	0430 （直播）女子職業高爾夫

Writing and Grammar

A Write the radical 扌 in the character 提 and three more characters with the same radical. Then compound each character with another one to form a disyllabic word or phrase, and provide their meanings in English (write the radical in 1).

1 _____

3 _____ _____

2 _____

4 _____

B Form a character by fitting the given components together as indicated, then provide a word or phrase in which that character appears. Follow the example below.

左邊一個"月"，右邊一個"土"是"肚子"的"肚"。

1 左邊一個"月"，右邊一個"半"是 ＿＿＿＿＿＿
的 ＿＿＿＿ 。

2 左邊一個"扌"，右邊一個"白"是 ＿＿＿＿＿＿
的 ＿＿＿＿ 。

3 左邊一個"扌"，右邊一個"是"是 ＿＿＿＿＿＿
的 ＿＿＿＿ 。

4 左邊一個"足"，右邊一個"易"是 ＿＿＿＿＿＿
的 ＿＿＿＿ 。

5 上邊一個"音"，下邊一個"心"是 ＿＿＿＿＿＿
的 ＿＿＿＿ 。

C Answer these questions according to your own workout routine. INTERPERSONAL

1 Q: 你喜歡什麼運動？

A: ＿＿＿＿＿＿＿＿＿＿＿＿＿＿＿＿＿＿＿＿＿＿＿

2 Q: 你常常去什麼地方運動？

A: ＿＿＿＿＿＿＿＿＿＿＿＿＿＿＿＿＿＿＿＿＿＿＿

3 Q: 你每個星期/每個月運動幾次？

A: ＿＿＿＿＿＿＿＿＿＿＿＿＿＿＿＿＿＿＿＿＿＿＿

4 Q: 你每次運動多長時間？

A: _____

5 Q: 你多長時間沒運動了？

A: _____

D Answer these questions according to your own circumstances. <u>INTERPERSONAL</u>

1 Q: 你的中文老師平常坐著上課還是站著上課？

A: _____

2 Q: 你常常坐著還是躺著聽音樂？

A: _____

3 Q: 你覺得抱著球跑累不累？

A: _____

E Look at this chart and summarize who did what for how long yesterday. Follow the example below.
PRESENTATIONAL

李友昨天打掃房子打掃了兩個小時/鐘頭。

or李友昨天打掃了兩個小時（的）房子。

1 _____

2 _____

3 _____

4 _____

5 _____

F Based on the images, write questions-and-answers to discuss the following situations.
Use 被/叫/讓 to indicate the passive voice in the answers, following the example below.
<u>PRESENTATIONAL</u>

Q: 蘋果呢？

A: 蘋果被人吃了。

1

Q: _____

A: _____

2

Q: _____

A: _____

3

Q: _____

A: _____

G Translate these sentences into Chinese. **PRESENTATIONAL**

1 **Student A:** The weather is getting colder and colder. You'd better put on some more clothes. Otherwise, you might catch a cold.

_____

Student B: Don't worry. I'm in great shape. I don't get sick easily.

_____

2 **Student A:** How come my tennis ball isn't round anymore?

_____

Student B: I'm sorry. It got crushed by the sofa.

_____

3 **Teacher:** Class, I have a fever. I'm going to have teach today's lesson sitting down.

_____

Student: Teacher, you should go home and rest.

_____

4 **Little Li:** Old Wang, do you know how to send text messages?

_____

Old Wang: I don't. I don't even know how to e-mail.

_____

Little Li: Old Wang, you don't even have a cell phone, right?

_____

Old Wang: Right!

_____

H Design a weekly workout schedule for yourself. For each workout session, indicate the type of exercise, location, frequency, and duration. **PRESENTATIONAL**

I Write a story based on the four images below. Make sure that your story has a beginning, middle, and end, and that the transition from one image to the next is smooth and logical. **PRESENTATIONAL**

_____

_____

_____

_____

_____

旅行
Travel

 Check off the following items as you learn them.

Useful Expressions

[ ] Time flies!

[ ] I haven't decided yet.

[ ] I'll apply for a visa.

[ ] Two one-way/round-trip tickets, please.

[ ] Can I make a reservation?

Cultural Norms

[ ] Rail travel

[ ] Major travel agencies

[ ] Major airlines

[ ] Attitudes toward travel

As you progress through the lesson, note other useful expressions and cultural norms you would like to learn.

_____

_____

_____

Dialogue 1: Traveling to Beijing

Audio

Listening Comprehension

A   Listen to the Textbook Dialogue 1 audio, then circle the most appropriate choice. INTERPRETIVE

1   **What's Wang Peng's plan for summer break?**

     a   to do an internship

     b   to visit his parents

     c   to take summer classes

     d   to get a part-time job

2   **At the beginning of the conversation, does Li You have summer plans?**

     a   No, nothing definite.

     b   Yes, she plans to get a part-time job.

     c   Yes, she plans to visit her parents.

     d   Yes, she plans to take summer classes.

3   **Wang Peng seems particularly proud of Beijing's many**

     a   good restaurants.

     b   important libraries.

     c   cultural centers.

     d   cool stores.

4   **If Li You wanted to leave for Beijing today, she wouldn't have to worry about getting**

     a   a passport and an airline ticket.

     b   a passport and a Chinese visa.

     c   a tour guide and an airline ticket.

     d   a passport and a tour guide.

B   Listen to the Workbook Dialogue audio, then mark these statements true or false. INTERPRETIVE

1   _____   The woman wants to go to northern California because she wouldn't have to speak a foreign language.

2   _____   The woman dislikes both flying and hot weather.

3   _____   The man doesn't think much of northern California, but the woman manages to persuade him of its charms.

4   _____   It seems that the woman has been to northern California before.

C   _____   Listen to the Listening Rejoinder audio. After hearing the first speaker, select the best response from the four choices given by the second speaker. Indicate the number of your choice below. Indicate the number of your choice. INTERPRETIVE

A Identify the characters with the same initials (either *j* or *zh*) and write them in *pinyin*.

際 蹟 治 計 直

1 *j:* _____

2 *zh:* _____

B Compare the tones of these characters. Indicate the tones with 1 (first tone), 2 (second tone), 3 (third tone), 4 (fourth tone), or 0 (neutral tone).

1 蹟 _____ 計 _____

2 證 _____ 政 _____

3 簽 _____ 前 _____

4 北 _____ 被 _____

Speaking

A Answer these questions in Chinese based on Textbook Dialogue 1. PRESENTATIONAL

1 What are Wang Peng's classmates' plans for the summer?

2 What is Wang Peng's plan for the summer?

3 What does Wang Peng say about Beijing?

4 Which cities in Asia has Li You visited before?

5 What does Li You need to do in order to travel to Beijing?

B In pairs, have a conversation about summer break. Ask your partner whether he/she plans to travel, work, study, or do something else over the break. INTERPERSONAL

C Search online to find out how long it takes and how much it costs to obtain a tourist visa to China. In pairs, compare notes on your findings. PRESENTATIONAL

A If you combine the *chūn* in *chūntiān* with the *jià* in *fàngjià*, you have *chūnjià*, as seen in exercise 1 below. Can you guess what the word *chūnjià* means? Write the characters, *pinyin*, and English equivalent of each new word formed in this way. Consult a dictionary if necessary. **INTERPRETIVE**

1 "春天"的"春"+"放假"的"假"

→ 春+假 → _____ _____ _____

2 "放假"的"放"+"擔心"的"心"

→ 放+心 → _____ _____ _____

3 "養寵物"的"養"+"父母"的"父"

→ 養+父 → _____ _____ _____

4 "訂機票"的"訂"+"押金"的"金"

→ 訂+金 → _____ _____ _____

5 "報紙"的"報"+"旅行社"的"社"

→ 報+社 → _____ _____ _____

B Read this dialogue, then mark the statements true or false. **INTERPRETIVE**

（還有三個星期學校就放假了。白英愛打算一放假就坐飛機回家去看爸爸媽媽，在家住三個星期，然後回學校。）

李友：英愛，飛機票買好了嗎？

白英愛：買好了。比上次回家的機票便宜不少。

李友：　是嗎？你是在哪家旅行社買的？

白英愛：是高文中幫我在網上買的，他說在網上買又快、又方便、又便宜。

李友：　英愛，我覺得高文中很不錯。你一點兒都不喜歡他嗎？

白英愛：我也不知道我喜歡不喜歡他。昨天他聽說我放假要回家，就給我打手機說要開車送我去機場。

李友：　那你跟他說什麼？

白英愛：我說，要是他真的那麼喜歡開車，等我回來以後，我跟他一起開車去加州實習吧。

李友：　哎，英愛，那他一定高興得不得了。太好了！

1 ____ Bai Ying'ai's summer break is only three weeks long.

2 ____ Bai Ying'ai plans to leave as soon as break starts.

3 ____ It wasn't hard for Bai Ying'ai to get a cheap flight.

4 ____ Gao Wenzhong will drive Bai Ying'ai to the airport.

5 ____ Bai Ying'ai probably does like Gao Wenzhong.

高小音：文中，學校要放假了，你有什麼
打算？上暑期班還是再去我們
圖書館打工？

高文中：不，我要和白英愛一起去加州
的一家公司實習。

高小音：是嗎？

高文中：我和白英愛都沒去過，可是我
看過不少加州的照片，漂亮得
不得了。

高小音：我去過加州好幾次，就是在加
州認識我男朋友的，所以我對
加州的印象特別好。

高文中：是嗎？你想不想再去一次加州？
當我們的導遊。

高小音：我當然想去，可是我工作太忙，
也沒有假。

高文中：那我和白英愛在那兒多照幾張
照片，用電子郵件或者短信發
給你吧。

1 ____ Gao Wenzhong has never worked at Gao Xiaoyin's library.

2 ____ Gao Wenzhong has been to California before.

3 ____ California holds a special place in Gao Xiaoyin's heart.

4 _____ Gao Xiaoyin wishes that she could go with Gao Wenzhong.

5 _____ Gao Wenzhong's tour guide will help them take a lot of photos.

D Look at this newspaper ad from a travel agency, then answer the questions. INTERPRETIVE

夢幻4重奏 香港大 FUN送

北京出發全綫航班+香港40家星級酒店+接送機/電話卡/地鐵票

1 Which city is the focus of this tour package?

_____

2 From which city does the tour leave?

_____

3 What's included in the package? List at least three things.

_____

E Look at this banner. What kind of advertisements are welcome (歡迎) (huānyíng) here? INTERPRETIVE

歡迎刊登
旅遊廣告

Writing and Grammar

A In addition to 實習, provide three more words that contain the character 習, along with the meaning of each of them in English.

1 _____ _____

2 _____ _____

3 _____ _____

4 _____ _____

B Answer these questions according to your own circumstances. INTERPERSONAL

1 Q: 學校幾月幾號開始放暑假？

   A: _____

2 Q: 暑假放多長時間？

   A: _____

3 Q: 暑假你打算做什麼？回家看父母、打工、出國旅行、在學校上暑期班，還是什麼都不做？

   A: _____

C Write the English names of the following airlines. Search online if necessary. INTERPRETIVE

1 美國航空公司 _____

2 英國航空公司（英航）_____

3 加拿大航空公司（加航）_____

4 日本航空公司（日航）_____

5 西南航空公司 _____

6 中國東方航空公司 _____

D Fill in the blanks with the appropriate information about these capitals, following the example below. **PRESENTATIONAL**

Washington, D.C. 是美國的首都，也是美國的政治中心。

1 北京 _____

2 東京 _____

3 紐約 _____

E Translate these sentences and the passage into Chinese. **PRESENTATIONAL**

1 Student A: Have you heard of the Great Wall?

_____

   Student B: Of course. The Great Wall is the most famous historic site in China. Everyone knows it. It's huge. Have you been to it?

_____

   Student A: I haven't.

_____

   Student B: I've been to the Great Wall many times. I'll take you there and be your tour guide.

_____

2 Time flies! Summer break is around the corner. Some of my classmates are interning at different companies. Some are going home to work. I'll be traveling to Tokyo. Tokyo is the capital and the political and cultural center of Japan, with many famous historic sites. There are too many good restaurants to count. I don't need a visa to go to Japan, and I have my airline ticket ready. I'm leaving the day after tomorrow. See you next semester.

_____

_____

_____

_____

F Write an essay about which cities you have visited, and which of those cities has given you the best impression. Explain why you like that city. Discuss the weather, the people, the shopping, the tourist sights, whether the city is a political or cultural center, etc. Alternatively, pick a city you would like to visit in the future and write about why you have a good impression of that city as a travel destination. PRESENTATIONAL

_____

_____

_____

_____

Dialogue 2: Planning an Itinerary

Audio

Listening Comprehension

A Listen to the Textbook Dialogue 2 audio, then mark these statements true or false. **INTERPRETIVE**

1 _____ Wang Peng and Li You are leaving for Beijing in early June.

2 _____ Wang Peng and Li You plan to stay in Beijing for about a month.

3 _____ Wang Peng doesn't put in seat requests for the flight to Beijing.

4 _____ Wang Peng asks for vegetarian meals for both himself and Li You.

5 _____ Because it's cheaper, Wang Peng decides to fly Air China.

B Listen to the Workbook Narrative audio, then mark these statements true or false. **INTERPRETIVE**

1 _____ Little Wang doesn't like flying because he thinks it's dangerous.

2 _____ Little Wang never feels that the cabin temperature is right.

3 _____ Little Wang often gets an upset stomach from eating airline food.

4 _____ Little Wang often misses his connections because he spends too much time at airport restaurants.

5 _____ Little Wang prefers to travel by car.

C _____ Listen to the Listening Rejoinder audio. After hearing the first speaker, select the best response from the four choices given by the second speaker. Indicate the number of your choice. **INTERPRETIVE**

Pinyin and Tone

A | Identify the characters with the same finals (either *an* or *ang*) and write them in *pinyin*.

往 返 餐 航 班

1 *an:* _____

2 *ang:* _____

B Compare the tones of these characters. Indicate the tones with 1 (first tone), 2 (second tone), 3 (third tone), 4 (fourth tone), or 0 (neutral tone).

1 初 _____ 廚 _____   3 份 _____ 分 _____

2 轉 _____ 專 _____   4 千 _____ 錢 _____

Speaking

A Answer these questions in Chinese based on Textbook Dialogue 2. PRESENTATIONAL

1 When is Wang Peng going back to Beijing this summer?

2 What's his strategy for deciding on an airline to fly?

3 Why does Wang Peng choose Air China?

4 Does Wang Peng ask for aisle or window seats?

5 What else does Wang Peng request?

B In pairs, role-play a conversation between a traveler and a travel agent. The traveler calls the travel agent to inquire about ticket prices from where he/she lives to Beijing, Hong Kong, or Taipei, telling the travel agent his/her departure and return dates, airlines of interest, and seat and meal preferences. The agent should present the passenger with several options. INTERPERSONAL

C In pairs, discuss a recent trip, your favorite trip, or a trip you would like to take in the future. Remember to mention the purpose of the trip, the dates, your transportation arrangements, your travel companions, the length of the trip, and any enjoyable or frustrating aspects of the trip. PRESENTATIONAL

Reading Comprehension

A If you combine the *dān* in *dānchéng* with the *hào* in *hàomǎ*, you have *dānhào*, as seen in exercise 1 below. Can you guess what the word *dānhào* means? Write the characters, *pinyin*, and English equivalent of each new word formed in this way. Consult a dictionary if necessary. INTERPRETIVE

1 "單程"的"單"+"號碼"的"號"

→ 單＋號 → _____ _____ _____

2 "往返"的"返"+"航班"的"航"

→ 返+航 → ＿＿＿＿＿＿　＿＿＿＿＿＿　＿＿＿＿＿＿

3 "直飛"的"飛"+"糖醋魚"的"魚"

→ 飛+魚 → ＿＿＿＿＿＿　＿＿＿＿＿＿　＿＿＿＿＿＿

4 "轉機"的"轉"+"學校"的"學"

→ 轉+學 → ＿＿＿＿＿＿　＿＿＿＿＿＿　＿＿＿＿＿＿

5 "快慢"的"快"+"素餐"的"餐"

→ 快+餐 → ＿＿＿＿＿＿　＿＿＿＿＿＿　＿＿＿＿＿＿

B Read this passage, then mark these statements true or false. INTERPRETIVE

　　小張和小藍是男女朋友。小張常常換工作，什麼工作錢多他就做什麼工作，哪兒的工作好他就去哪兒住。他十個月前從北京搬到香港，可是在香港只住了半年多，就在上海找到了一個錢更多的工作。小藍跟他不一樣，對錢沒有興趣，哪個城市有文化，她喜歡哪個城市，所以她一直住在北京，哪兒也不想搬。小張說他每個星期都要坐飛機去北京看一次小藍，把錢都花在飛機票上了，希望以後能兩個星期飛一次。小藍說要是小張愛她，又不想花錢，很簡單，搬回北京。要不然，就再見。

1 _____ Little Zhang has lived in three different cities in the past year.

2 _____ Little Zhang wants to experience life in different big cities.

3 _____ Little Zhang makes more money now than he did months ago.

4 _____ Little Lan is staying put because she has a well-paid job where she is.

5 _____ Little Zhang is not happy about spending money on airline tickets.

6 _____ Little Lan has given Little Zhang an ultimatum.

C Review Teacher Gao's travel itinerary, then answer the questions. INTERPERSONAL

Holiday Tours 假期旅遊

```
12 JUN - WEDNESDAY
  UNITED        1547 COACH CLASS
  LV: SEATTLE            941A      NONSTOP              CONFIRMED
  AR: SAN FRANCISCO     1145A
  SNACK-AUDIO                       SEAT-15D

  UNITED         857 COACH CLASS
  LV: SAN FRANCISCO      135P      NONSTOP              CONFIRMED
  AR: SHANGHAI/PUDON     540P      ARRIVAL DATE-13 JUN
  LUNCH-LUNCH-MOVIE                 SEAT-47C

12 JUN - FRIDAY
  CHINA EASTER 5161 COACH CLASS
  LV: SHANGHAI/PUDON     345P      NONSTOP              CONFIRMED
  AR: BEIJING            545P
  SNACK

22 JUN - SATURDAY
  UNITED         852 COACH CLASS
  LV: BEIJING            925A      NONSTOP              CONFIRMED
  AR: TOKYO/NARITA       150P
  LUNCH                            SEAT-34B

  UNITED         876 COACH CLASS
  LV: TOKYO/NARITA       455P      NONSTOP              CONFIRMED
  AR: SEATTLE            930A
  DINNER-BREAKFAST-MOVIE           SEAT-35A
```

1 Q: 你知道不知道高老師的飛機票是什麼時候
訂的？

A: _____

2 Q: 你知道不知道飛機票是多少錢買的？

A: _____

3 Q: 高老師的飛機票是跟旅行社還是跟航空公司訂的？

A: _____

4 Q: 高老師哪一天走？從哪兒走？

A: _____

5 Q: 高老師到什麼地方去？

A: _____

6 Q: 高老師哪一天回美國？

A: _____

7 Q: 他回美國的航班號碼是多少？

A: _____

8 Q: 他買的是往返票還是單程票？

A: _____

9 Q: 高老師去中國的時候坐的是直飛的飛機嗎？

A: _____

10 Q: 位子訂好了嗎？

A: _____

11 Q: 旅行社的中文名字叫什麼？

A: _____

D Answer these questions based on the menu. INTERPRETIVE

1 On a flight between which two cities will this meal be served?

_____

2 Is this meal suitable for vegetarians? Why or why not?

_____

3 What beverages are on offer?

_____

_____

午餐/晚餐

香港 – 北京

日本芥末蘋果雜菜沙拉

黑椒汁扣牛肉配白飯
或
紅酒燴豬柳配意大利麵

哈根達斯雪糕

麵包、牛油

誠意提供　太平洋咖啡

福茗堂茶莊
福建烏龍、福建特級香片

紅茶、日本綠茶

E Look at the ad, then answer the questions. INTERPRETIVE

1 Name two items that are on sale.

_____

2 On which day of the week is the discount available?

_____

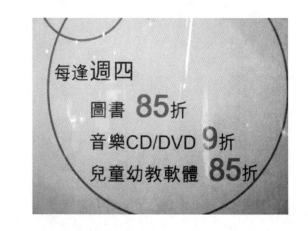

F Look at this ad, then answer the questions.

1 Circle baby bok choy. If the original price of baby bok choy was $1, what would the sale price be?

_____

2 What does 有機 mean?

_____ (Hint: 有機 vegetables are more expensive than regular vegetables.)

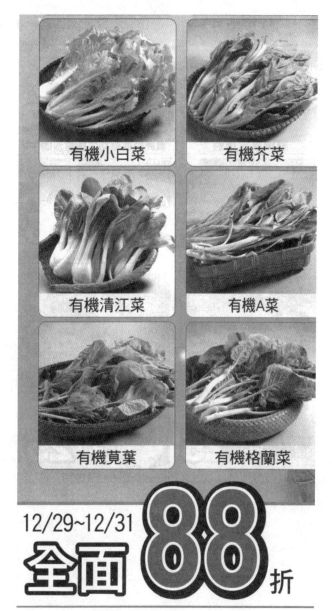

有機小白菜　　有機芥菜

有機清江菜　　有機A菜

有機莧葉　　有機格蘭菜

12/29~12/31 全面 88 折

G Look at this travel agency ad, then name as many of the services they provide as you can.

酒店　　機票　　旅遊　　商旅

Writing and Grammar

A Write the radical 衤 in the character 初 (beginning) and three more characters with the same radical. Then compound each character with another one to form a word or short sentence, and provide their meanings in English (write the radical in 1).

1

2 _____ _____

3 _____ _____

4 _____ _____

B Form a character by fitting the given components together as indicated, then provide a word or phrase in which that character appears. Follow the example.

左邊一個"土"，右邊一個"成"是"長城"的"城"。

1 上邊一個"戶"，下邊一個"方"是 _____ 的 _____ 。

2 左邊一個"氵"，右邊一個"台"是 _____ 的 _____ 。

3 上邊一個"夕"，下邊一個"口"是 _____ 的 _____ 。

4 左邊一個"車"，右邊一個"專"是 _____ 的 _____ 。

5 上邊一個"告"，下邊一個"非"是 _____ 的 _____ 。

C Search online to find out the populations of these cities, then write them down in Chinese, following the example below. **PRESENTATIONAL**

香港 (about 7,500,000)

香港差不多有七百五十萬人。

1 台北 _____

2 上海 _____

3 北京 _____

4 紐約 _____

5 東京 _____

6 我現在住的城市 _____

D 請把出國旅行以前得做的事、得準備或者得帶的東西寫出來： **PRESENTATIONAL**

1 _____

2 _____

3 _____

4 _____

5 _____

6 _____

7 _____

8 _____

E List the prices of the following items from two stores in Chinese, then compare those prices, following the example below. PRESENTATIONAL

兩千三百元/塊錢

$2300

兩千一百元/塊錢

$2100

這個商店的電視比那個商店的電視貴兩百元/塊錢。

那個商店的電視比這個商店的電視便宜兩百元/塊錢。

1　　　

$1500　　　　$1560

_____　　　_____

_____

_____

2

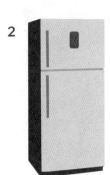

$850

$750

_____

_____

_____

3

$109

$115

_____

_____

_____

F Based on the prompts and images, express the discount being offered, following the example below. **PRESENTATIONAL**

Then: $100   Now: $80

這件衣服打八折。

1    Then: $20   Now: $15

_____

2    Then: $50   Now: $25

_____

3   Then: $200   Now: $180

_____

G Translate these sentences into Chinese. **PRESENTATIONAL**

1 **Student A:** Where would you like to sit?

_____

Student B: I'll sit wherever you want to sit.

_____

Student A: Let's sit next to the window. What would you like to drink?

_____

Student B: I'll have whatever you order.

_____

Student A: What kind of dishes would you like to have?

_____

Student B: I'll eat anything.

_____

2 Student A: I heard that airline tickets are on sale.

_____

Student B: I'll go online and check right now.

_____

Student A: Twenty percent off or thirty percent off?

_____

Student B: The online ad says that if you buy a round-trip ticket, the second round-trip ticket will be fifty percent off.

_____

_____

Student A: Then forget it.

_____

H You are a travel agent. Having just helped a customer plan her trip and book a flight with Southwest Airlines, you recap the itinerary with her in Chinese, since she doesn't understand English. Be as detailed as possible and include information such as the times and places of her departures and arrivals, the route she is taking, how long each flight will take, the airline she is taking, the flight numbers, whether the tickets are one-way or round-trip, whether the flights are nonstop, etc. (Note that Chicago is 芝加哥 *[Zhījiāgē]* and Los Angeles is 洛杉磯 *[Luòshānjī]*.) **PRESENTATIONAL**

Trip	Date	Day	Stops	Routing	Flight	Routing Details
Depart	Jul 15	Sat	N/S	MDW-LAX	971	Depart Chicago (MDW) at 1:05 p.m. Arrive in Los Angeles (LAX) at 3:20 p.m.
Return	Aug 04	Fri	N/S	LAX-MDW	723	Depart Los Angeles (LAX) at 10:20 a.m. Arrive in Chicago (MDW) at 4:15 p.m.

_____

_____

_____

I Write a story based on the four images below. Make sure that your story has a beginning, middle, and end, and that the transition from one picture to the next is smooth and logical. PRESENTATIONAL

1

2

3

4
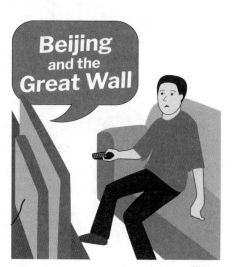

_____

_____

_____

_____

_____

在機場

At the Airport

 Check off the following items as you learn them.

Useful Expressions

[ ] Please show me your passport.

[ ] I'd like to take this luggage on board.

[ ] Have a safe trip!

[ ] Have fun!

[ ] Welcome to Beijing!

Cultural Norms

[ ] Travel expressions

[ ] Beijing airports

[ ] Beijing roast duck

As you progress through the lesson, note other useful expressions and cultural norms you would like to learn.

_____

_____

_____

Dialogue 1: Checking in at the Airport

Audio

Listening Comprehension

A Listen to the Textbook Dialogue 1 audio, then circle the most appropriate choice. INTERPRETIVE

1 How many people see Wang Peng and Li You off at the airport?

   a two

   b three

   c four

   d five

2 When do Wang Peng and Li You finish checking in?

   a around 9:00 a.m.

   b around 10:00 a.m.

   c around 11:00 a.m.

   d around 12:00 p.m.

3 What will Bai Ying'ai do while Wang Peng and Li You are traveling?

   a She will intern in New York.

   b She will go back home.

   c She will go to California with Gao Wenzhong.

   d She will join Wang Peng and Li You in Beijing.

4 What will Wang Hong do while Wang Peng and Li You are traveling?

   a She will be on her own.

   b She will be with Gao Xiaoyin.

   c She will travel with Gao Wenzhong and Bai Ying'ai.

   d She will go back to China in a few weeks.

B Listen to the Workbook Narrative audio, then mark these statements true or false. INTERPRETIVE

1 _____ The plane has already taken off.

2 _____ The flight is from Beijing to Shanghai.

3 _____ The plane will arrive at the destination at 3:00 p.m.

4 _____ Because the flight is so short, no snacks or beverages will be served.

C _____ Listen to the Listening Rejoinder audio. After hearing the first speaker, select the best response from the four choices given by the second speaker. Indicate the number of your choice. INTERPRETIVE

Pinyin and Tone

A | Identify the characters with the same initials (either *x* or *zh*) and write them in *pinyin*.

行 照 重 折 箱

1 *x:* _____

2 *zh:* _____

B | Compare the tones of these characters. Indicate the tones with 1 (first tone), 2 (second tone), 3 (third tone), 4 (fourth tone), or 0 (neutral tone).

1 包 _____ 抱 _____

2 箱 _____ 象 _____

3 機 _____ 際 _____

4 哭 _____ 酷 _____

Speaking

A | Answer the questions in Chinese based on Textbook Dialogue 1. PRESENTATIONAL

1 How many pieces of luggage does Wang Peng check?

2 Where should Wang Peng and Li You go to board the plane?

3 Why does Wang Hong sound worried?

4 What will Bai Ying'ai do this summer?

5 What does Li You say when she learns about Bai Ying'ai and Gao Wenzhong's summer plans?

6 What does Bai Ying'ai tell Wang Peng and Li You to do when they arrive in Beijing?

B | In Chinese, what do people usually say when they see friends off? PRESENTATIONAL

C | In pairs or groups, role-play seeing friend(s) off at a local airport. Make small talk right before the departure of your friend(s). INTERPERSONAL

A If you combine the *shū* in *shūdiàn* with *bāo*, you have *shūbāo*, as seen in exercise 1 below. Can you guess what the word *shūbāo* means? Write the characters, *pinyin*, and English equivalent of each new word formed in this way. Consult a dictionary if necessary. **INTERPRETIVE**

1 "書店"的"書"+"包"

→ 書+包 → _____ _____ _____

2 "超重"的"超"+"汽車"的"車"

→ 超+車 → _____ _____ _____

3 "超重"的"超"+"高速公路"的"速"

→ 超+速 → _____ _____ _____

4 "汽車"的"車"+"登機牌"的"牌"

→ 車+牌 → _____ _____ _____

5 "出去"的"出"+"登機口"的"口"

→ 出+口 → _____ _____ _____

B Read this passage, then mark the statements true or false. **INTERPRETIVE**

　　今天白英愛坐飛機回學校。她托運了一件大行李，然後帶著一個小包、護照和登機牌到九號登機口上飛機。上了飛機以後，白英愛剛在自己的位子上坐下，就聽到航空公司的一位女服務員跟大家說："這是去紐約的521號航班。要是您上錯了飛機，請您趕快下飛機。”她剛說完，坐在白英愛旁邊的兩位先生就說：“不對！我們的航班是去紐約的，可是是531號！”女服務員聽了以後，就到飛機的前邊去了。五分鐘以後，她才回來對大家說：“真對不起，你們是對的，這是531號航班。電腦壞了，所以我上錯飛機了。”

1 ____ Bai Ying'ai has two pieces of baggage.

2 ____ Bai Ying'ai goes to the wrong boarding gate.

3 ____ The men sitting next to Bai Ying'ai realize that they have boarded the wrong airplane.

4 ____ Both Flight 521 and Flight 531 are bound for New York.

5 ____ We can assume that Bai Ying'ai will not see that flight attendant again during her flight.

C | Read this dialogue, then mark the statements true or false. INTERPRETIVE

高文中：英愛！

白英愛：文中！等了很久吧？飛機一個小時以前就到了，可是我等托運的行李，等了半天了還沒等到。

高文中：真的？航空公司一定是把你的行李放錯飛機了。別擔心，他們會找到的。

白英愛：他們告訴我行李到了會給我打電話，要我等他們的電話。還好，我的信用卡、護照、錢，都在這個小包裡，要不然就麻煩了。下一班飛機是兩點半到，我想我的包一定在那個飛機上。我們還得等一個多小時。

高文中：那我們找個地方喝點咖啡吧。你知道嗎，李友後天要跟王朋一起去北京。

白英愛：是嗎？那我們後天可以去送他們。對了，我還沒告訴李友我們要去加州，她可能以為我要去紐約實習呢。

……

（航空公司的電話）：白英愛小姐嗎？非常對不起，我們剛查到您托運的行李，您的行李現在正在去東京的飛機上……

1 _____ 白英愛的航班早到了一個小時。

2 _____ 白英愛花了兩個半小時找她的行李，可是沒有找到。

3 _____ 高文中覺得白英愛的行李在別的飛機上。

4 _____ 白英愛很擔心她托運的包，因為她的護照在那個包裡。

5 _____ 白英愛早就知道李友要和王朋一起去北京。

6 _____ 李友還不知道白英愛最新的暑假計劃。

7 _____ 白英愛一個多小時以後能拿到她托運的行李。

D Review this notice posted at an airport. Is it meant to help people locate baggage carousels, airline check-in counters, or boarding gates? **INTERPRETIVE**

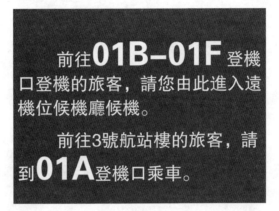

前往**01B–01F**登機口登機的旅客，請您由此進入遠機位候機廳候機。

前往3號航站樓的旅客，請到**01A**登機口乘車。

Writing and Grammar

A Write the radical ⺮ in the character 箱 and three more characters with the same radical. Then compound each character with another one to form a word or phrase, and provide their meanings in English (write the radical in 1).

1 _____ _____

2 _____ _____ _____

3 _____ _____ _____

4 _____ _____ _____

Fill in the blanks with 的, 得, or 地. **INTERPRETIVE**

暑假快到了，大家都高高興興＿＿＿準備放假，有的人打算去旅行，有的人打算去實習。但也有的人什麼事都不想做，只想好好兒＿＿＿在家休息休息。

希望每個人＿＿＿暑假都過＿＿＿很好，下個學期再見。

C Based on the images, use 把 to write instructions for moving these pieces of furniture out of your apartment, following the example below. **PRESENTATIONAL**

請把椅子搬出房間去。

1

_____

2

_____

3

_____

D Fill in the blanks with 的時候 or 以後 as appropriate. **INTERPRETIVE**

1 生病＿＿＿＿＿＿，別亂跑，得在家休息。

2 父母死了＿＿＿＿＿＿，都是大哥照顧我們。

3 開車＿＿＿＿＿＿，別打手機，太危險了。

4 行李超重＿＿＿＿＿＿得多付錢。

5 簽證辦好＿＿＿＿＿＿，就可以訂機票了。

E Translate these sentences into Chinese. **PRESENTATIONAL**

1 **Student A:** Be careful. It's dangerous here. Don't run around.

＿＿＿＿＿＿＿＿＿＿＿＿＿＿＿＿＿＿＿＿＿＿＿＿

Student B: Don't worry. I'm sitting right here.

＿＿＿＿＿＿＿＿＿＿＿＿＿＿＿＿＿＿＿＿＿＿＿＿

2 **Student A:** Don't forget to send me an e-mail when you get to Tokyo.

＿＿＿＿＿＿＿＿＿＿＿＿＿＿＿＿＿＿＿＿＿＿＿＿

Student B: OK . . . Don't cry. I'll be back in a month. Study hard at school.

＿＿＿＿＿＿＿＿＿＿＿＿＿＿＿＿＿＿＿＿＿＿＿＿

Student A: OK. Bye. Have fun.

＿＿＿＿＿＿＿＿＿＿＿＿＿＿＿＿＿＿＿＿＿＿＿＿

F Plan a trip to China: after choosing two cities in China that you would like to visit, explain your interest in these two cities, then arrange a trip from your current location. Search online for information about the cities, airfares, and hotel accommodations, and put together a travel itinerary with information on flights, airlines, airfares, how long it will take to get to each destination and how long you plan to spend there, your transportation to and from the airports, errands you need to take care of before you depart, and things you need to take with you on the trip. Don't forget to keep an eye on your budget. **PRESENTATIONAL**

_____

_____

_____

_____

G Your friend from China is traveling in the U.S. and needs your help understanding airline policies. Use the information below to fully explain the luggage policies on this particular airline to your friend. (Note that pound is 磅 [bàng].) **PRESENTATIONAL**

Domestic Free Luggage Allowance
Each ticketed passenger traveling domestically is allowed one piece of checked luggage and one piece of carry-on luggage, plus a purse or briefcase or laptop case. All checked and carry-on luggage is subject to the following limitations:

Checked Luggage
The Airline will accept checked luggage up to a maximum weight of 50 pounds (23 kg). Luggage weighing between 50 and 70 pounds (23–32 kg) will be assessed $25 USD per piece and luggage weighing between 70 and 100 pounds (32–46 kg) will be assessed $50 USD per piece. Luggage weighing over 100 pounds (46 kg) will not be accepted as checked luggage.

Carry-On Luggage
Each person is allowed one piece of carry-on luggage not exceeding 40 pounds, and one personal item such as a purse, briefcase, or backpack.

_____

_____

_____

_____

Dialogue 2: Arriving in Beijing

Listening Comprehension

🔊
Audio

A Listen to the Textbook Dialogue 2 audio, then mark these statements true or false. INTERPRETIVE

1 _____ Wang Peng's grandparents are waiting in a car outside the airport terminal.

2 _____ Wang Peng's parents are impressed with Li You's Chinese.

3 _____ Wang Peng has lost some weight due to his busy schedule.

4 _____ Wang Peng's parents plan to take Wang Peng and Li You directly home.

B Listen to the Workbook Narrative audio of a voice mail Li You left for her father from Beijing, then circle the most appropriate choice. INTERPRETIVE

1 **Where is Li You calling from?**

a a roast duck restaurant

b an airport terminal

c Wang Peng's parents' apartment

d the car leaving the airport

2 **Li You promises to**

a call her dad again tomorrow.

b catch up on her sleep.

c buy a cell phone for her dad.

d buy some DVDs for her dad.

3 **Which statement is correct?**

a Li You is very tired.

b Li You is already homesick.

c Li You is impressed with Beijing Capital Airport.

d Li You is very impatient.

4 **To call, Li You uses**

a Wang Peng's cell phone.

b Wang Peng's dad's cell phone.

c Wang Peng's mom's cell phone.

d her own cell phone.

C _____ Listen to the Listening Rejoinder audio. After hearing the first speaker, select the best response from the four choices given by the second speaker. Indicate the number of your choice. INTERPRETIVE

A Identify the characters with the same finals (either *u* or *ou*) and write them in *pinyin*.

叔 瘦 首 受 暑

1 *u:* _____

2 *ou:* _____

B Compare the tones of these characters. Indicate the tones with 1 (first tone), 2 (second tone), 3 (third tone), 4 (fourth tone), or 0 (neutral tone).

1 瘦 _____ 首 _____

2 叔 _____ 屬 _____

3 應 _____ 迎 _____

4 歡 _____ 換 _____

Speaking

A Answer the questions in Chinese based on Textbook Dialogue 2. PRESENTATIONAL

1 How does Li You address Wang Peng's parents?

2 How does Li You account for her Chinese language skills?

3 Why does Wang Peng's mother think Wang Peng has lost weight?

4 What does Wang Peng say about how Wang Hong is doing in the United States?

5 Where are Wang Peng's grandparents?

B How would you respond to a compliment on your Chinese? PRESENTATIONAL

C In groups, role-play traveling with a Chinese friend and meeting his/her parent for the first time at an airport in Mainland China or Taiwan. Address your host parent appropriately and express your feelings about your flight. The Chinese friend should make sure to introduce everyone. The parent should ask you about the trip, what you would like to do on your visit, etc. INTERPERSONAL

Reading Comprehension

A If you combine the *kǎo* in *kǎoyā* with the *ròu* in *niúròu*, you have *kǎoròu*, as seen in exercise 1 below. Can you guess what the word *kǎoròu* means? Write the characters, *pinyin*, and English equivalent of each new word formed in this way. Consult a dictionary if necessary. **INTERPRETIVE**

1 "烤鴨"的"烤"+"牛肉"的"肉"

→ 烤+肉 → ＿＿＿＿＿＿＿ ＿＿＿＿＿＿＿ ＿＿＿＿＿＿＿

2 "烤鴨"的"烤"+"箱子"的"箱"

→ 烤+箱 → ＿＿＿＿＿＿＿ ＿＿＿＿＿＿＿ ＿＿＿＿＿＿＿

3 "烤鴨"的"鴨"+"蛋糕"的"蛋"

→ 鴨+蛋 → ＿＿＿＿＿＿＿ ＿＿＿＿＿＿＿ ＿＿＿＿＿＿＿

4 "一塊錢"的"錢"+"包"

→ 錢+包 → ＿＿＿＿＿＿＿ ＿＿＿＿＿＿＿ ＿＿＿＿＿＿＿

5 "上海"的"海"+"托運"的"運"

→ 海+運 → ＿＿＿＿＿＿＿ ＿＿＿＿＿＿＿ ＿＿＿＿＿＿＿

王朋的妹妹王紅來美國找王朋的時候,她的爸爸、媽媽、爺爺和奶奶都到機場去送她。因為王紅的行李太多了,她爸爸的車放不下,所以爸爸跟媽媽開他們自己的車,王紅跟爺爺奶奶坐出租汽車去機場。這是王紅第一次出國,所以爸爸媽媽都很擔心,一直告訴她到美國以後要好好照顧自己。媽媽要王紅一到美國就讓哥哥給家裡打電話。王紅知道哥哥在美國一年了,有很多朋友,他們會照顧她的。她真不懂爸爸媽媽為什麼這麼擔心。

1 _____ 王紅去美國的時候不是坐爸爸的車去機場的。

2 _____ 王紅去美國以前去過一次日本。

3 _____ 王朋比王紅早一年去美國。

4 _____ 王紅到美國以後就會打電話給爸爸媽媽。

5 _____ 王紅出國,爸爸媽媽比王紅自己更擔心。

王紅在高小音家住了三個月了,英文水平提高了不少。王紅說都是因為小音教得好,可是小音說是因為王紅聰明。為了謝謝小音照顧自己，王紅計劃秋天請小音跟她一起去北京，帶小音看看北京的名勝古蹟，當小音的導遊，還要請她吃北京烤鴨。為了準備去中國，小音這幾天每天都跟王紅說中文，希望自己中文越來越好，秋天去中國什麼都聽得懂，什麼都會說。

1 ＿＿＿ Wang Hong is modest about the progress she has made in her English studies.

2 ＿＿＿ Gao Xiaoyin is dissatisfied with the progress Wang Hong has made in English.

3 ＿＿＿ Wang Hong wants to go back to Beijing in the fall because she's homesick.

4 ＿＿＿ Wang Hong plans to hire a tour guide for Gao Xiaoyin.

5 ＿＿＿ Gao Xiaoyin believes she can now understand and say anything in Chinese.

D Review this poster, then write the *pinyin* for the Chinese sentence.

Writing and Grammar

A Write the radical 疒 in the character 瘦 and three more characters with the same radical. Then compound each character with another one to form a word or phrase, and provide their meanings in English (write the radical in 1).

1 [grid box]

2 [grid box] _____ _____

3 [grid box] _____ _____

4 [grid box] _____ _____

B Form a character by fitting the given components together as indicated, then provide a word or phrase in which that character appears. Follow the example below.

左邊一個"力"，右邊一個"口"是"加州"的"加"。

1 上邊一個"木"，下邊一個"子"是 _____ 的 _____ 。

2 左邊一個"豸"，右邊一個"包"是 _____ 的 _____ 。

3 左邊一個"亻"，右邊一個"牛"是 _____ 的 _____ 。

4 上邊一個"田"，下邊一個"糸"是 _____ 的 _____ 。

5 左邊一個"火"，右邊一個"考"是 _____ 的 _____ 。

Answer these questions in Chinese according to your own circumstances. **INTERPERSONAL**

1 Q: 要是在機場或者車站送人，你會說些什麼話？

A: _____

_____

_____

2 Q: 要是在機場或者車站接人，你會說些什麼話？

A: _____

_____

_____

D Translate these sentences into Chinese. **PRESENTATIONAL**

1 **Student A:** You've worked for more than ten hours. You must be exhausted.

_____

Student B: I'm all right.

_____

Student A: You haven't had any food for eight hours. You must be starving.

_____

Student B: I'm OK.

_____

2 **Student A:** I eat whatever you eat and drink whatever you drink. How come I'm getting fatter and fatter and you're getting thinner and thinner?

_____

Student B: I exercise two or three times a week. How about you? You haven't exercised for two years.

E Translate this email sent by Wang Peng to Wang Hong into Chinese. PRESENTATIONAL

Sister:

　　We arrived in Beijing yesterday afternoon. We waited a long time for our checked luggage. Mom and Dad came to the airport to pick us up. Li You and I felt all right. We weren't too tired. As soon as we got out of the airport, we headed straight for a Peking duck restaurant for dinner. When we arrived at the restaurant, Grandma and Grandpa were already there. I hadn't had Peking duck for a long time, and enjoyed the food very much. Li You is a vegetarian, so she didn't have duck, and only had some vegetable dumplings. She ate faster than Grandma and Grandpa, and after she finished her food, she said in Chinese to Grandma and Grandpa: "Take your time with the food." I think Grandma and Grandpa were happy after hearing that.

Your brother

_____

_____

_____

_____

_____

_____

_____

_____

F Use the images to help you describe what people normally do: 1) one month before traveling overseas, 2) the night before flying out, and 3) on the day of travel. PRESENTATIONAL

1 _____

2 _____

3 _____

G Pick a tourist/historic site in Beijing or another major Chinese-speaking city that you would like to visit. Search online for information on the site, and write a simple tourist pamphlet with information on where it is located (east, south, west, or north of the city), how far it is from the airport, what transportation people can use to get there, why it is famous, etc. Don't forget to provide the characters and *pinyin* for the name of the site. PRESENTATIONAL

H Draw your family tree and list your family members and close relatives in Chinese. Use Grammar 5 in the textbook as a reference to complete the tree. **PRESENTATIONAL**

I Write a story in Chinese based on the four images below. Make sure that your story has a beginning, middle, and end, and that the transition from one image to the next is smooth and logical. PRESENTATIONAL

1

2

3

4

_____

_____

_____

_____

_____

Bringing It Together (Lessons 16–20)

A   Compare the characters' pronunciation and tones, then write them in *pinyin*.

1   我們倆 _____   我們兩個 _____

2   出租 _____   廚房 _____

3   傢俱 _____   公寓 _____

4   不准 _____   不瘦 _____

5   導遊 _____   游泳 _____

6   書架 _____   暑假 _____

Radicals

A   Group these characters according to their radicals.

架   初   簡   特   跑   胖   椅   被

籃   物   桌   腳   踢   簽   棒   臉

Radical	Characters
1 _____	_____
2 _____	_____
3 _____	_____

4 _____ _____

5 _____ _____

6 _____ _____

Characters

A Circle the common character in each group of words. Write down the *pinyin* for the character in common, then define its original meaning. For a challenge, see if you can think of any other words that contain the common character.

1 天氣　力氣 _____ _____

2 一定　一言為定 _____ _____

3 房間　衛生間 _____ _____

4 房間　房租 _____ _____

5 預報　報紙 _____ _____

6 最近　附近 _____ _____

7 分鐘　鐘頭 _____ _____

8 教室　臥室 _____ _____

9 請客　客廳 _____ _____

10 餐廳　客廳 _____ _____

11 暑期班　暑假 _____ _____

12 禮物　寵物 _____ _____

13 發燒　發短信 ＿＿＿＿＿＿＿＿＿＿　＿＿＿＿＿＿＿＿＿＿

14 水平　平安 ＿＿＿＿＿＿＿＿＿＿　＿＿＿＿＿＿＿＿＿＿

15 平安　安靜 ＿＿＿＿＿＿＿＿＿＿　＿＿＿＿＿＿＿＿＿＿

16 網上　網球 ＿＿＿＿＿＿＿＿＿＿　＿＿＿＿＿＿＿＿＿＿

17 保險　危險 ＿＿＿＿＿＿＿＿＿＿　＿＿＿＿＿＿＿＿＿＿

18 高興　興趣 ＿＿＿＿＿＿＿＿＿＿　＿＿＿＿＿＿＿＿＿＿

19 有名　名勝古蹟 ＿＿＿＿＿＿＿＿＿＿　＿＿＿＿＿＿＿＿＿＿

20 暑假　放假 ＿＿＿＿＿＿＿＿＿＿　＿＿＿＿＿＿＿＿＿＿

21 辦法　怎麼辦 ＿＿＿＿＿＿＿＿＿＿　＿＿＿＿＿＿＿＿＿＿

22 城市　中國城 ＿＿＿＿＿＿＿＿＿＿　＿＿＿＿＿＿＿＿＿＿

23 簡單　單程 ＿＿＿＿＿＿＿＿＿＿　＿＿＿＿＿＿＿＿＿＿

24 告訴　廣告 ＿＿＿＿＿＿＿＿＿＿　＿＿＿＿＿＿＿＿＿＿

25 走路　走道 ＿＿＿＿＿＿＿＿＿＿　＿＿＿＿＿＿＿＿＿＿

26 運動　托運 ＿＿＿＿＿＿＿＿＿＿　＿＿＿＿＿＿＿＿＿＿

27 喜歡　歡迎 ＿＿＿＿＿＿＿＿＿＿　＿＿＿＿＿＿＿＿＿＿

28 起床　起飛 ＿＿＿＿＿＿＿＿＿＿　＿＿＿＿＿＿＿＿＿＿

29 公司　公園 ＿＿＿＿＿＿＿＿＿＿　＿＿＿＿＿＿＿＿＿＿

30 練習　實習 ＿＿＿＿＿＿＿＿＿＿　＿＿＿＿＿＿＿＿＿＿

A Circle the verbs that are VO compounds.

打掃　整理　旅行　做飯　走路　游泳

跑步　放假　實習　打工　轉機　托運

Communication

A Interview one of your classmates and jot down the information you gather, then present an oral or written report to introduce him/her to others.

Sports and Exercise

1 你對什麼運動有興趣？

2 你對什麼球賽有興趣？

3 你平常運動嗎？

✔ a 你每個星期運動幾次？每次運動多長時間？

✖ b 你多長時間沒運動了？

4 你覺得什麼運動最簡單？為什麼？

5 你覺得什麼運動最麻煩？為什麼？

6 你覺得什麼運動最危險？為什麼？

Housing

1 你住的地方是宿舍、公寓、還是房子？住得下三個人嗎？

2 你住的地方幾房幾廳？有沒有自己的廚房、衛生間？

3 你住的地方帶不帶傢俱？有什麼傢俱？

4 你覺得你的房間乾淨嗎？你常常整理房間嗎？

5 你每個月打掃幾次房子？

6 這個地方對你合適嗎？為什麼？

7 你打算住下去還是搬出去？為什麼？

Travel

1 你去過哪些城市/國家？

2 你對哪一個城市/國家的印象最好/最糟糕？

3 你是什麼時候去的？怎麼去的？

4 你在那兒玩兒了多長時間？

5 你還會再去一次嗎？

6 如果你有錢、有時間，你希望能到什麼地方去旅行？

7 要是坐飛機，你怎麼訂票？你跟旅行社、航空公司訂機票，還是上網訂機票？

A Beijing and New York City are both world-renowned cities. Search online and find out more about them. Compare the two: how similar or different are they? You can do all six tasks or choose just a few. Report your findings to the class.

1 Check tomorrow's weather forecast for the two cities. Determine which one will be warmer or colder and whether it's supposed to rain tomorrow in either city.

2 Compare the population of the two and determine which city has more people.

3 Find out what means of public transportation are available in each city and determine which public transportation system is more convenient. Figure out where the international airports are located in relation to the downtown area, and how to get there.

4 List today's currency exchange rate for US dollars and RMB. Find out how much a watermelon, a refrigerator, and a basketball would cost in a local store in each city. Compare the prices in the two cities.

5 List today's currency exchange rate for US dollars and RMB. Find out how much it would cost to rent an apartment with two bedrooms and one bathroom in each city.

6 Find one US airline and one Chinese airline that provide flight service between the two cities. Describe their routes, departure times, flight durations, airfares, how many meals they serve onboard, etc. Compare the two options, and decide which airline you would like to fly.